POSTCARDS...

a coloring book for creative grown-ups

Illustrated by:

MENUCHA CITRON CEDER

a creative grown-up

ISBN: 978-0-9980794-3-1

Visit momsandcrafters.com for free printable samples, exclusive coloring pages, coloring tips, craft tutorials and more, and to learn more about the author. Membership is free.

INTRODUCTION

Far away places... Beautiful scenes... Special foods... Your own backyard.

It's long ago been determined that pretty things belong on... postcards. If you're going to keep your note that short, the other side has got to be beautiful, no?

Postcards is about seeing the beauty in everything around you.
It's about those far away places, that vacation on the beach.

But it's also about that cardinal perched on your mailbox on a snowy day, while you imagine the beautiful silhouettes of those snowflakes.
It's about nature's beauty and about man-made beauty.
It's about that imaginary paradise, and the real sunset.

So step right in and add your own color.

I've created these images in full size so that you can get the most out of them. But I've also offered them in smaller postcard-like sizes at the end, in case you really DO want to mail them out. Just cut it out, glue to cardstock, or to a blank postcard, after you've colored it.

Note: some of the postcard size images feature extremely fine detail. Don't worry about filling in every little dot - look at the bolder outline. I left the fine detail there because it creates a beautiful texture.

I hope these pretty pictures truly brighten your day!

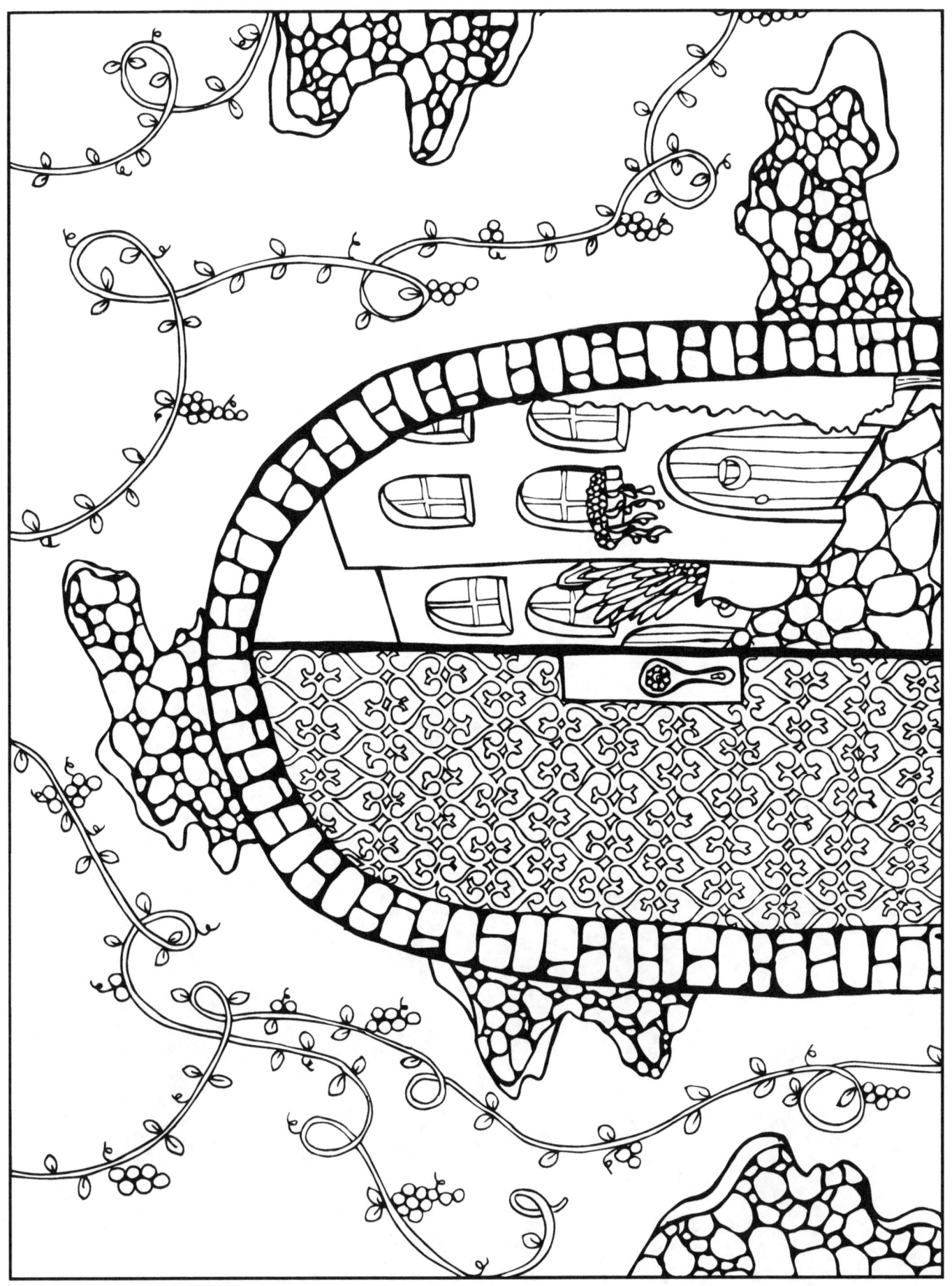

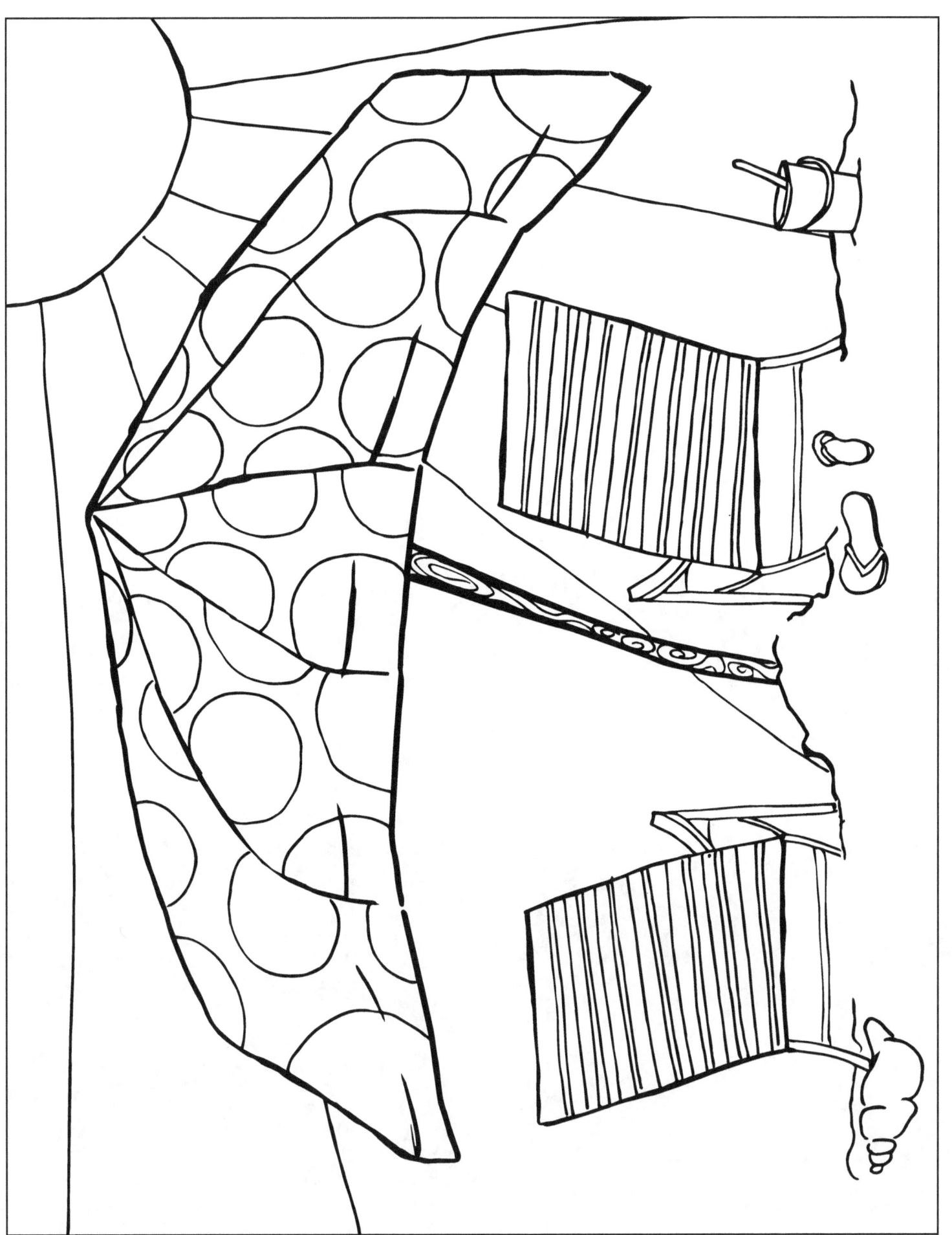

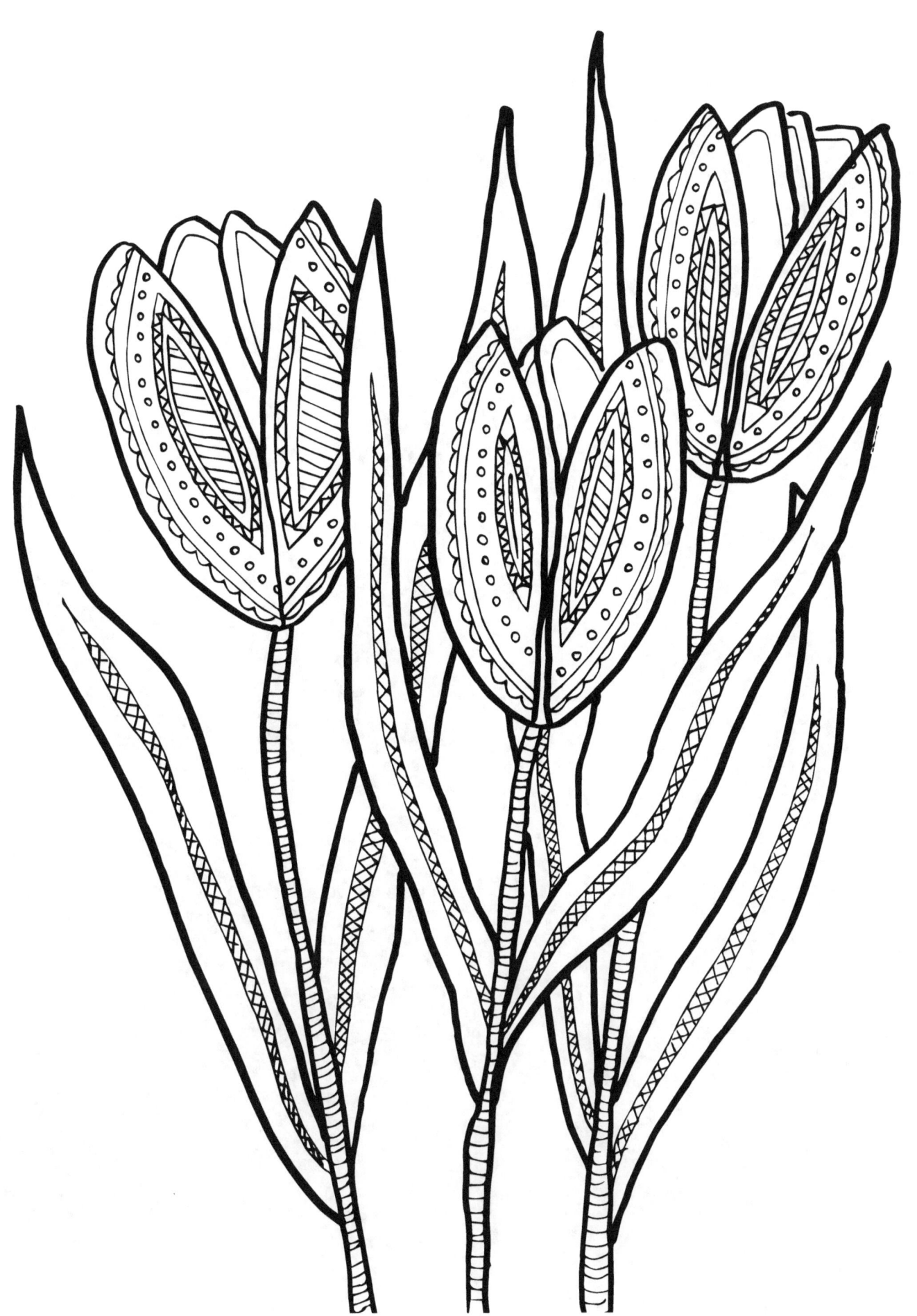

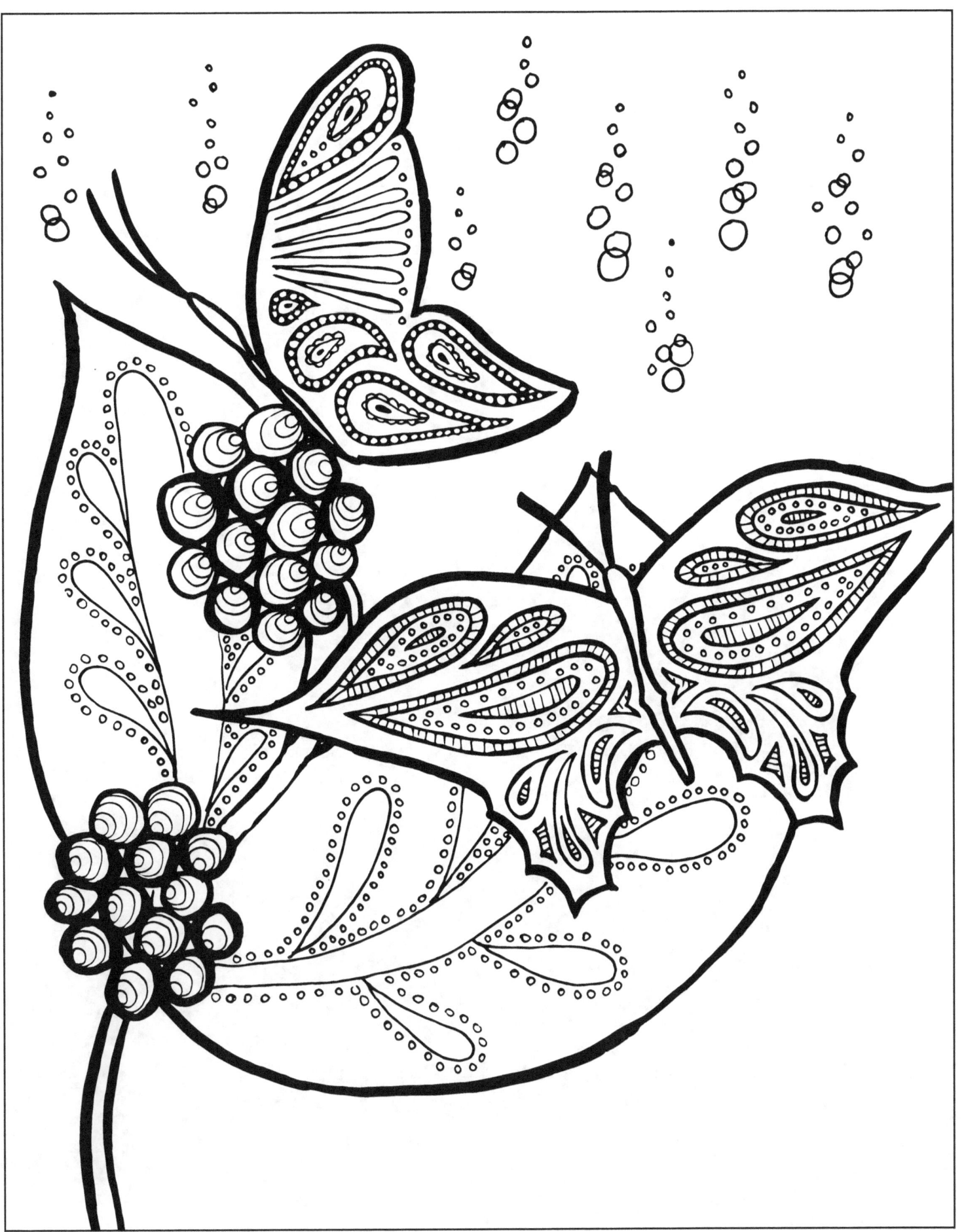

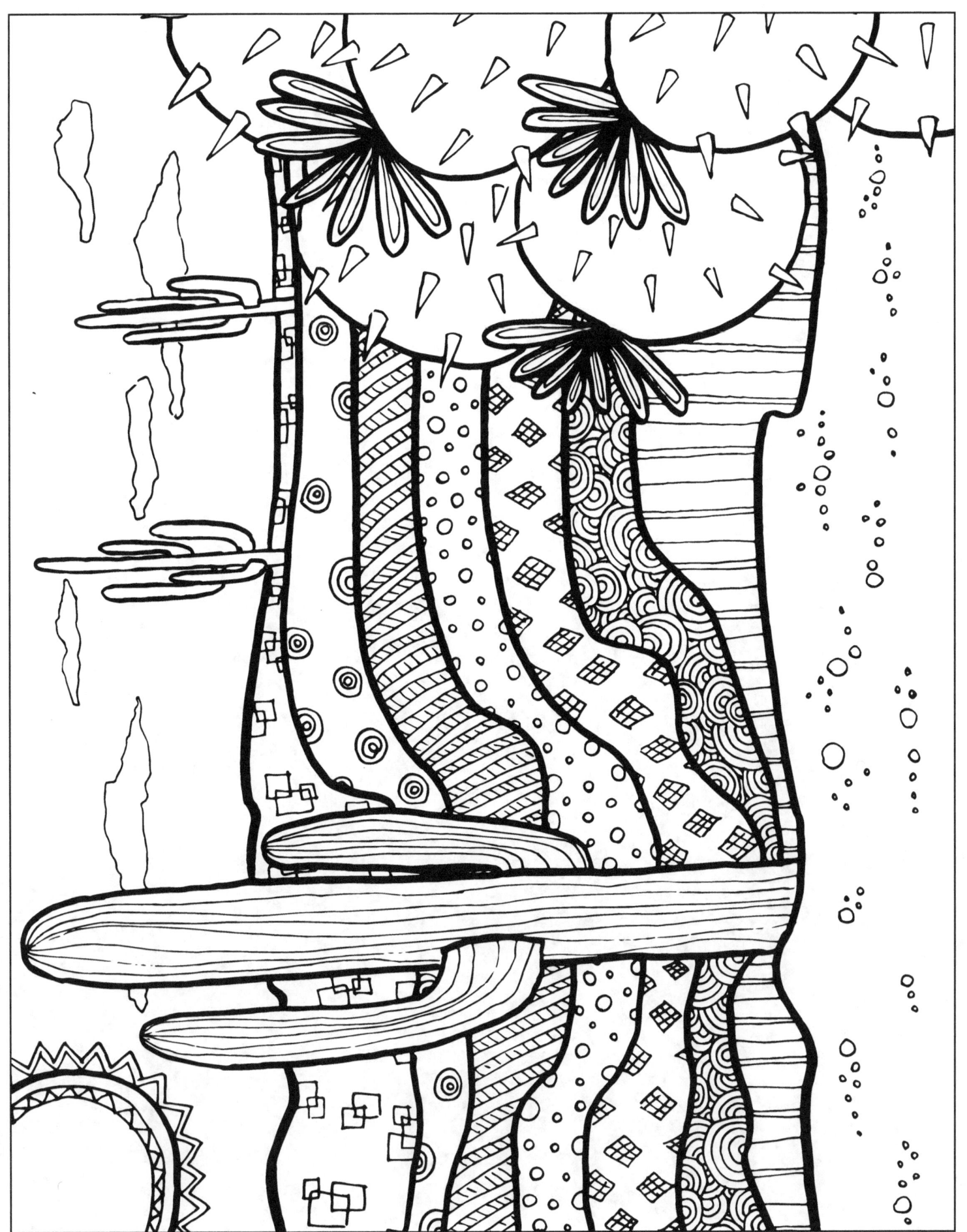

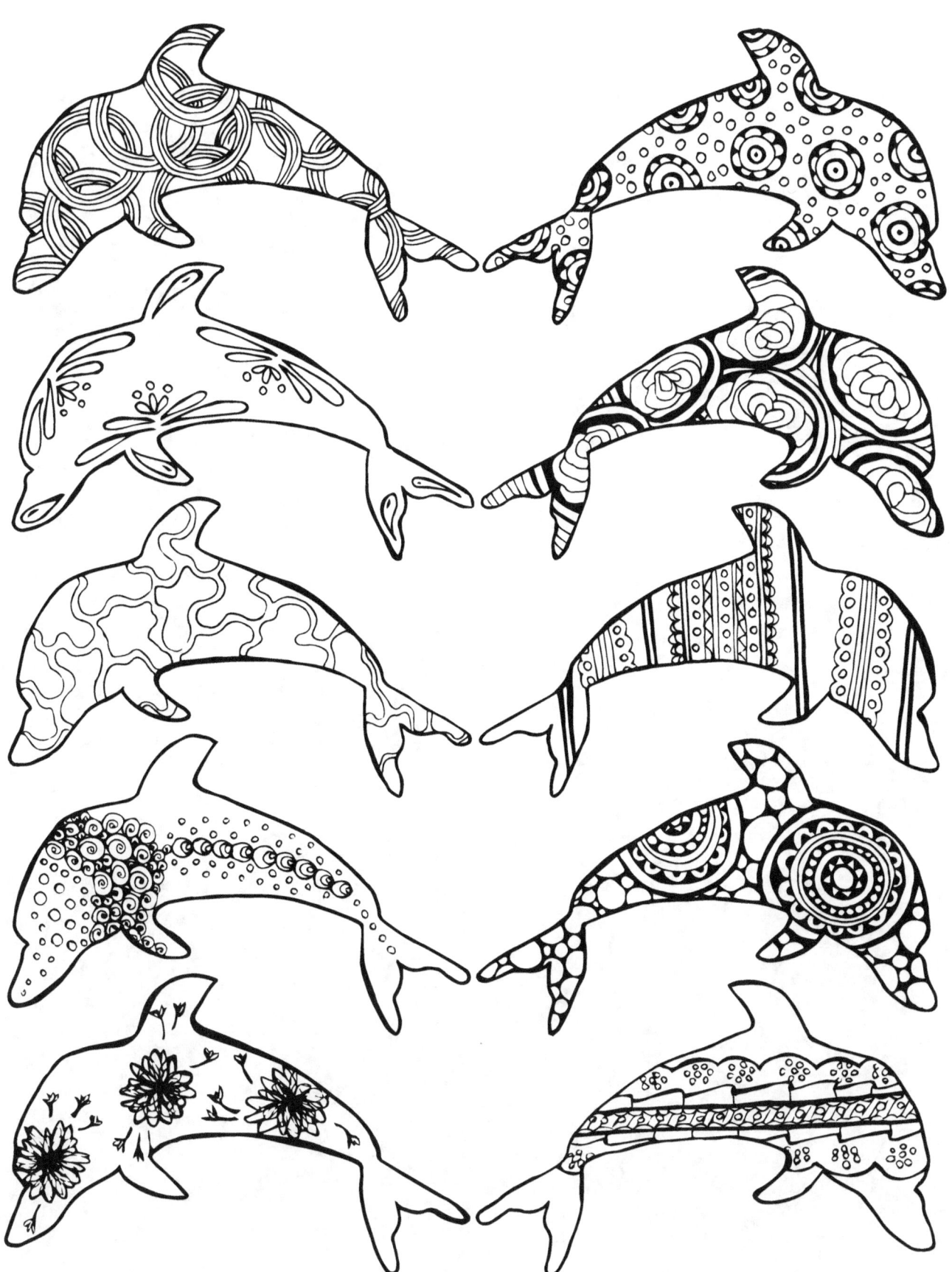

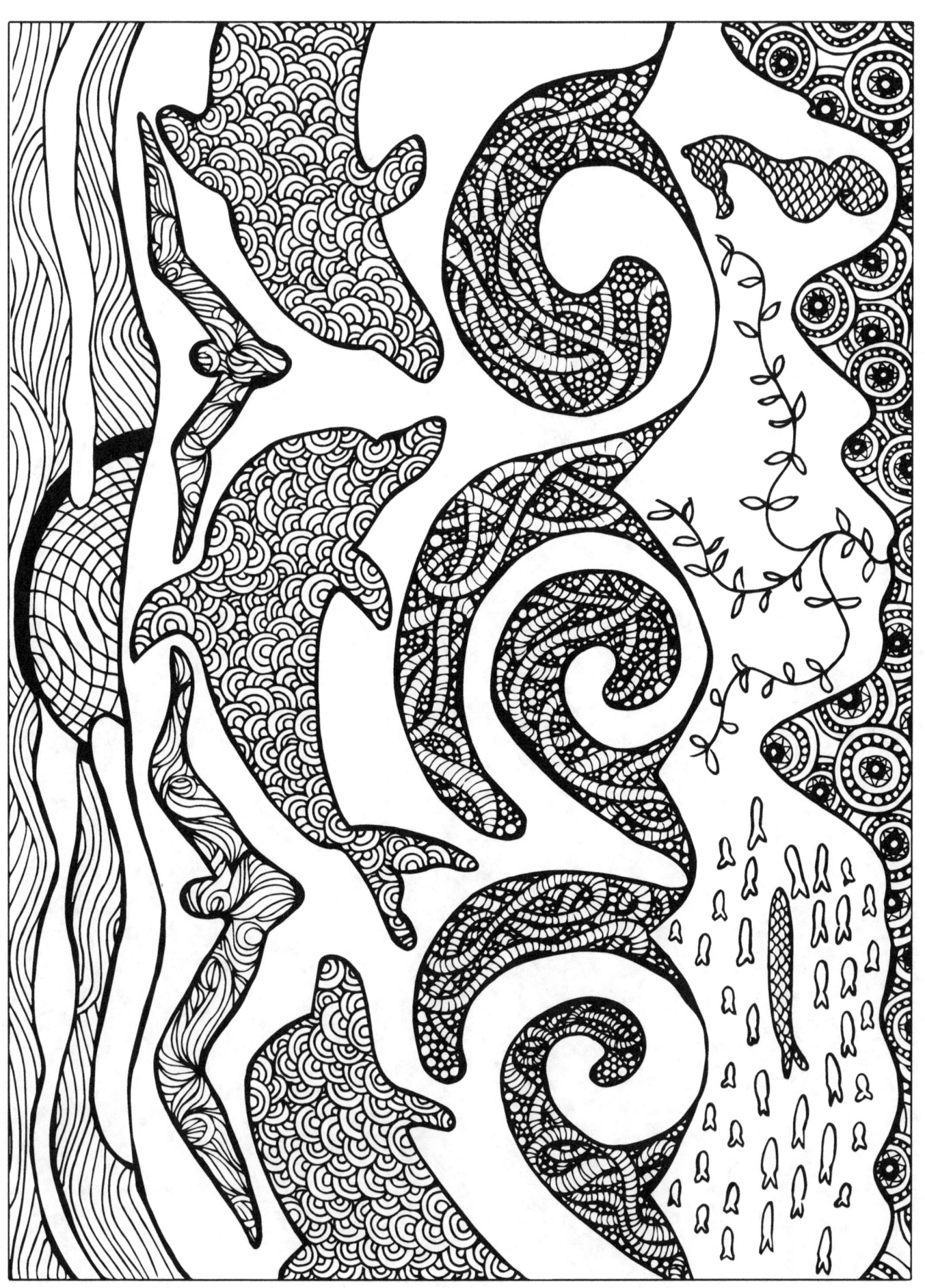

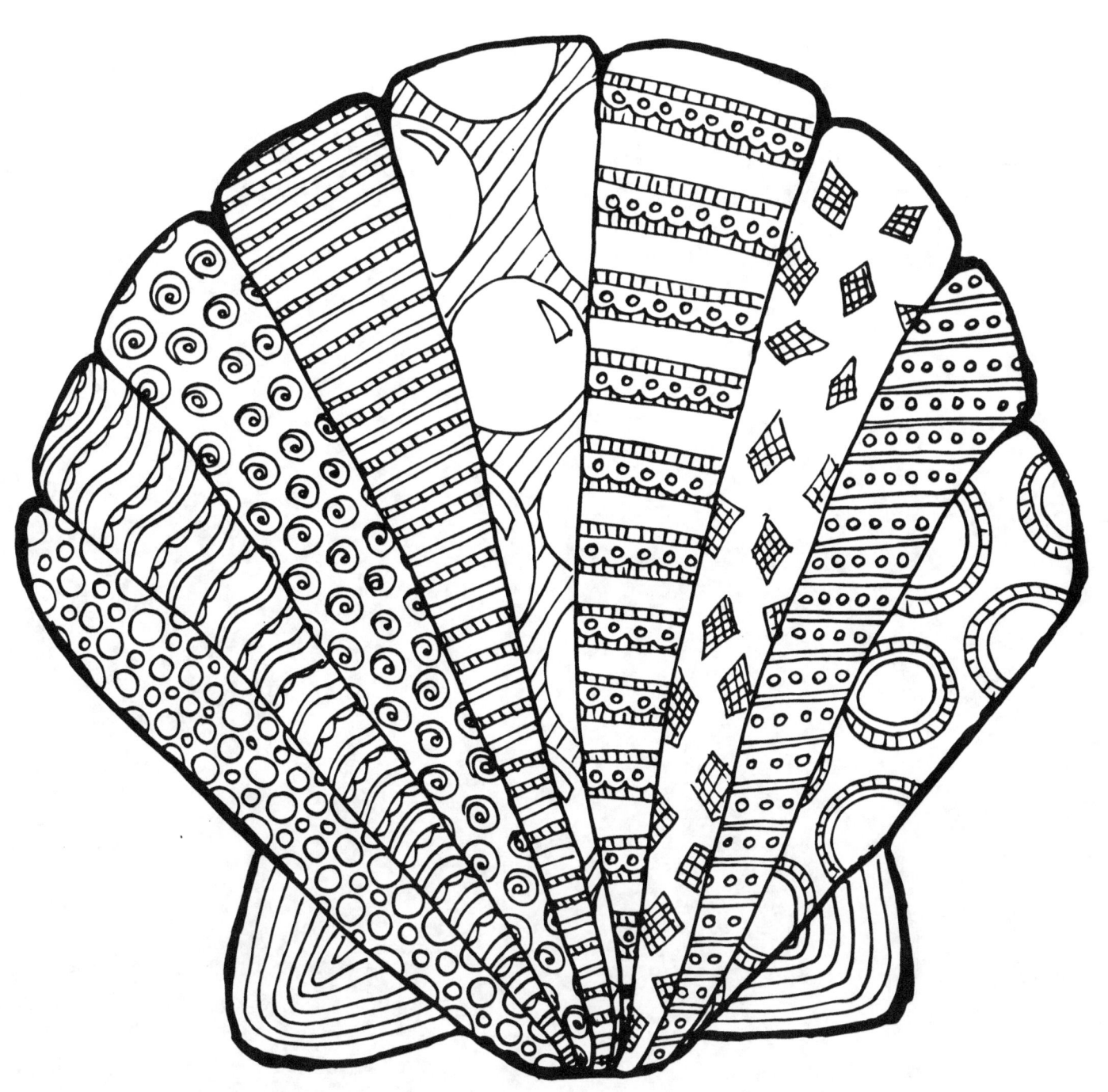

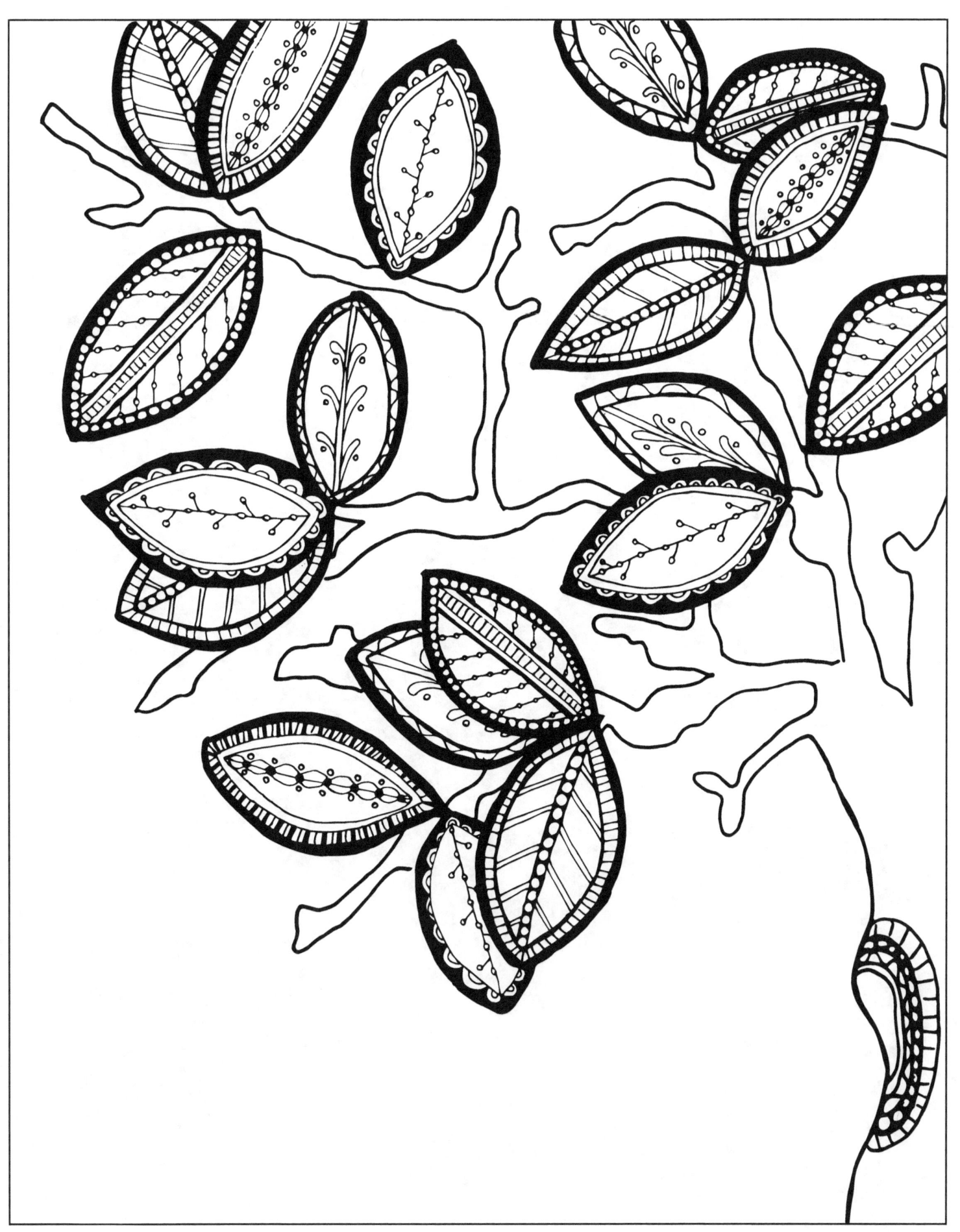

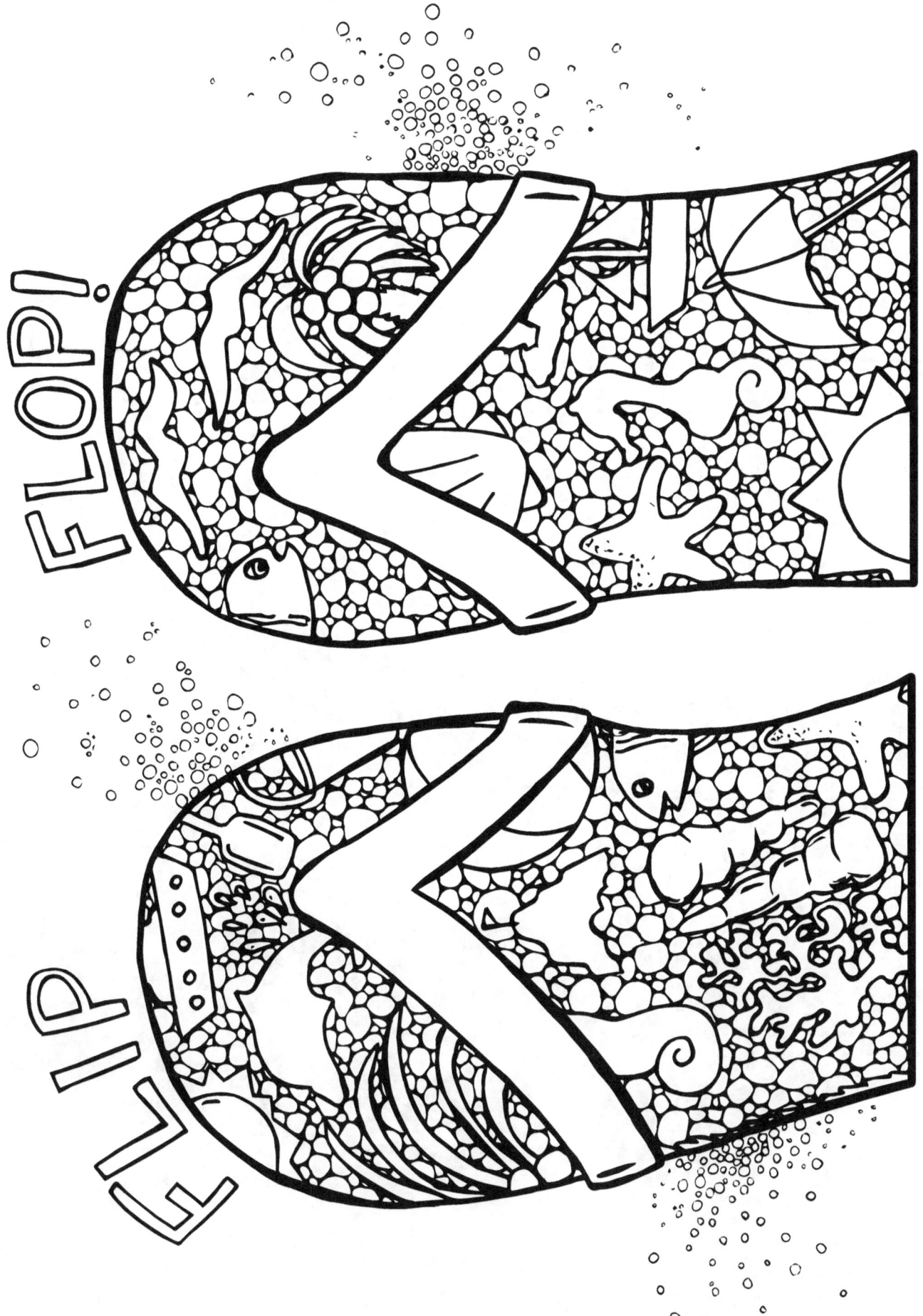

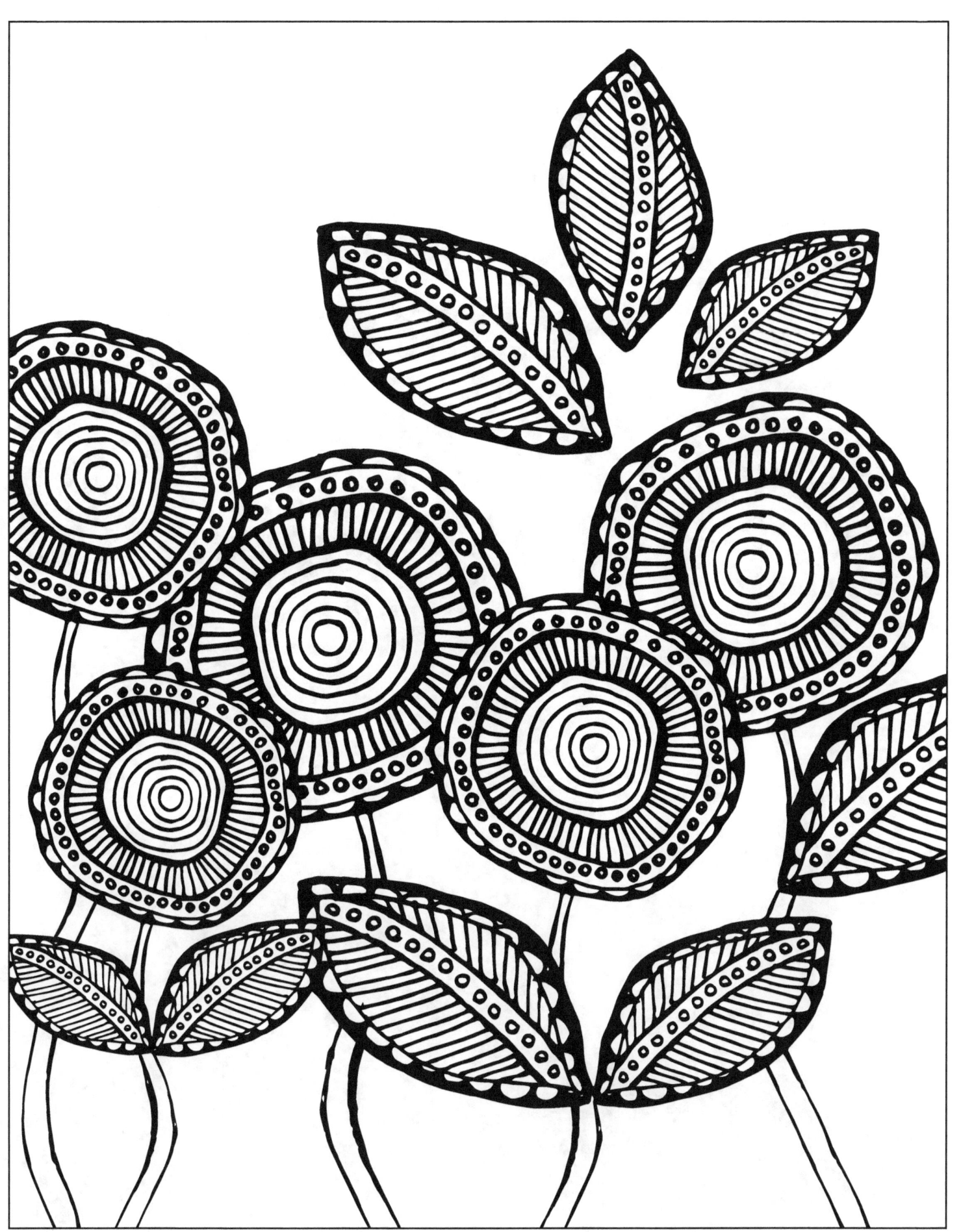

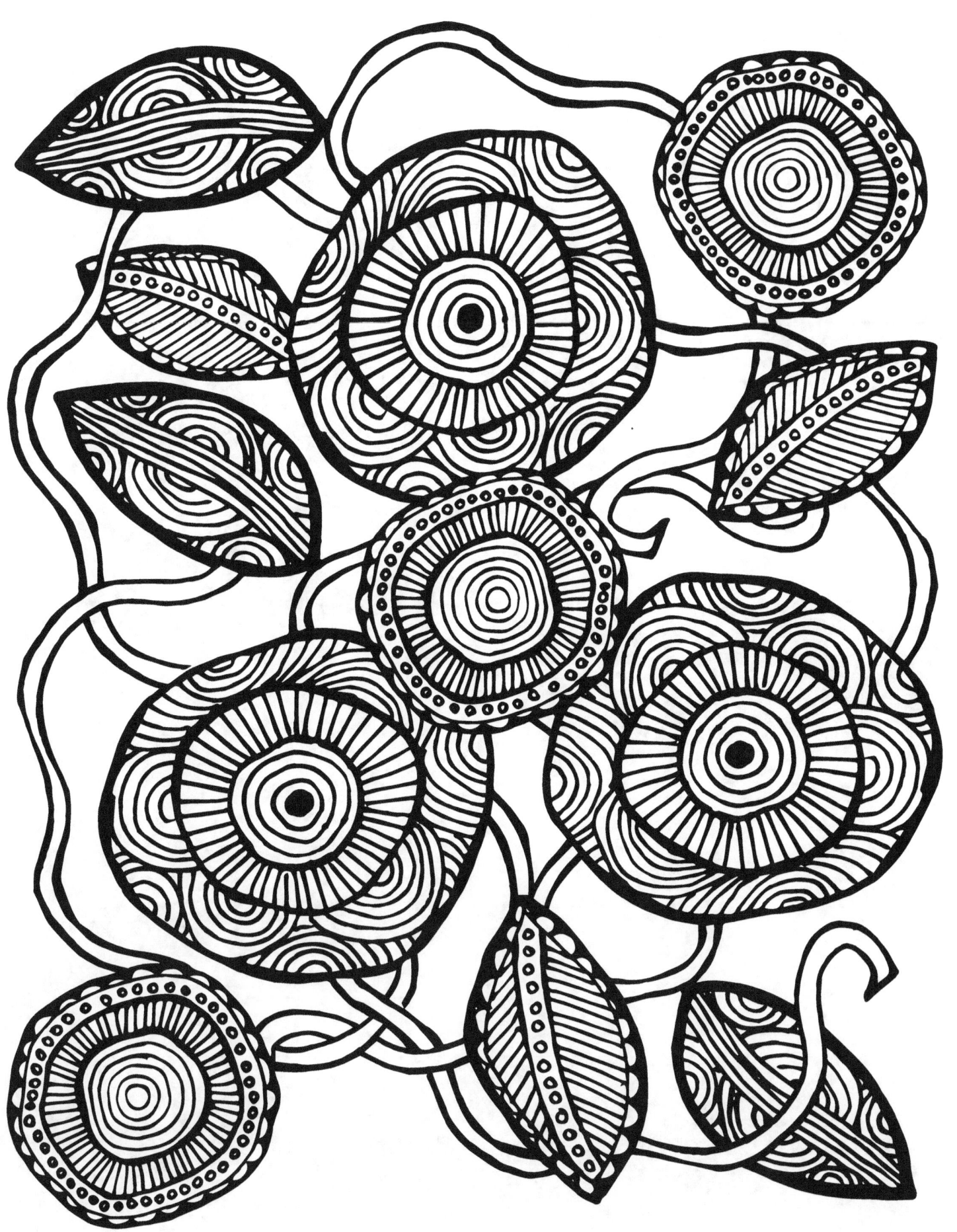

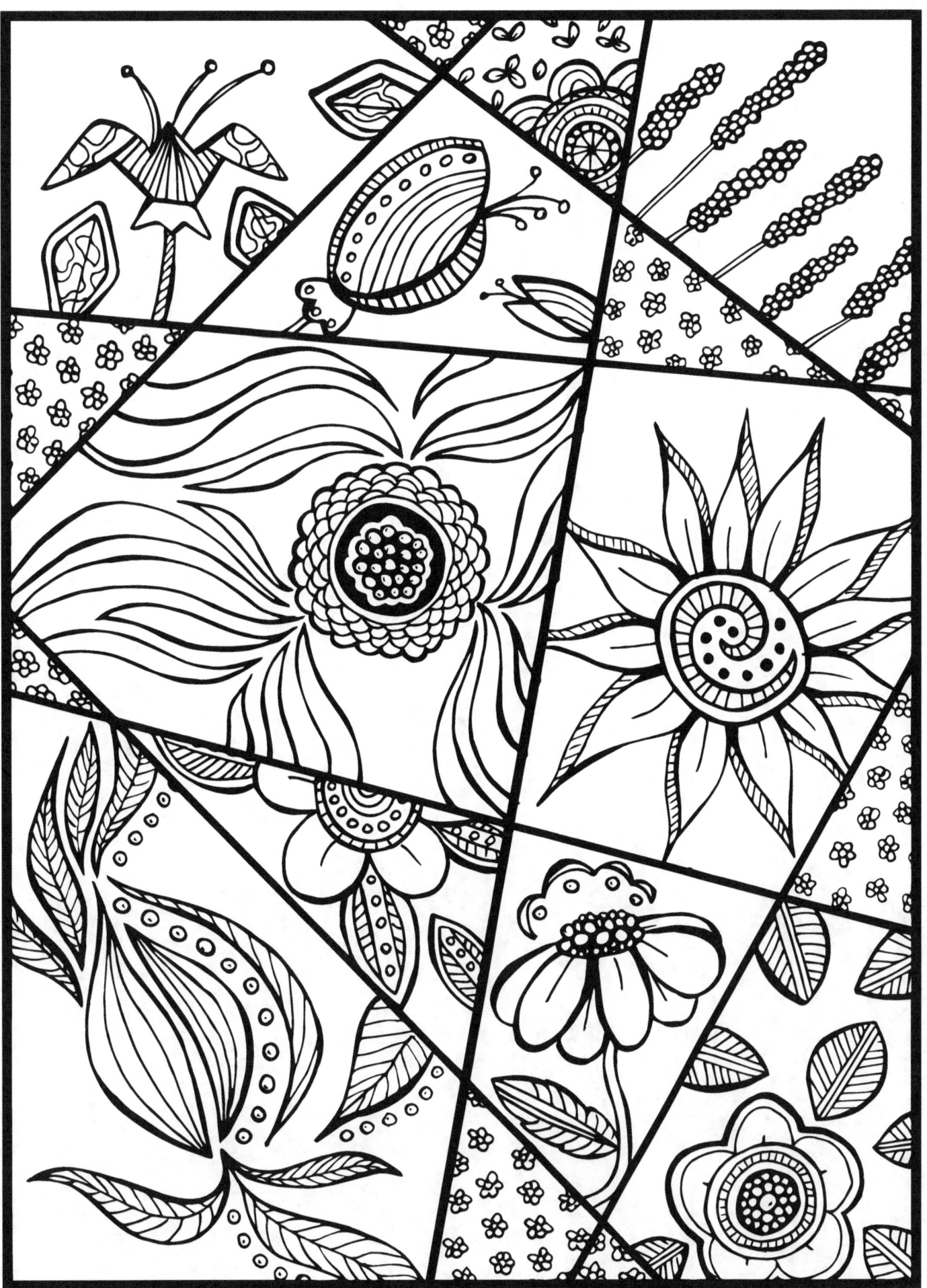

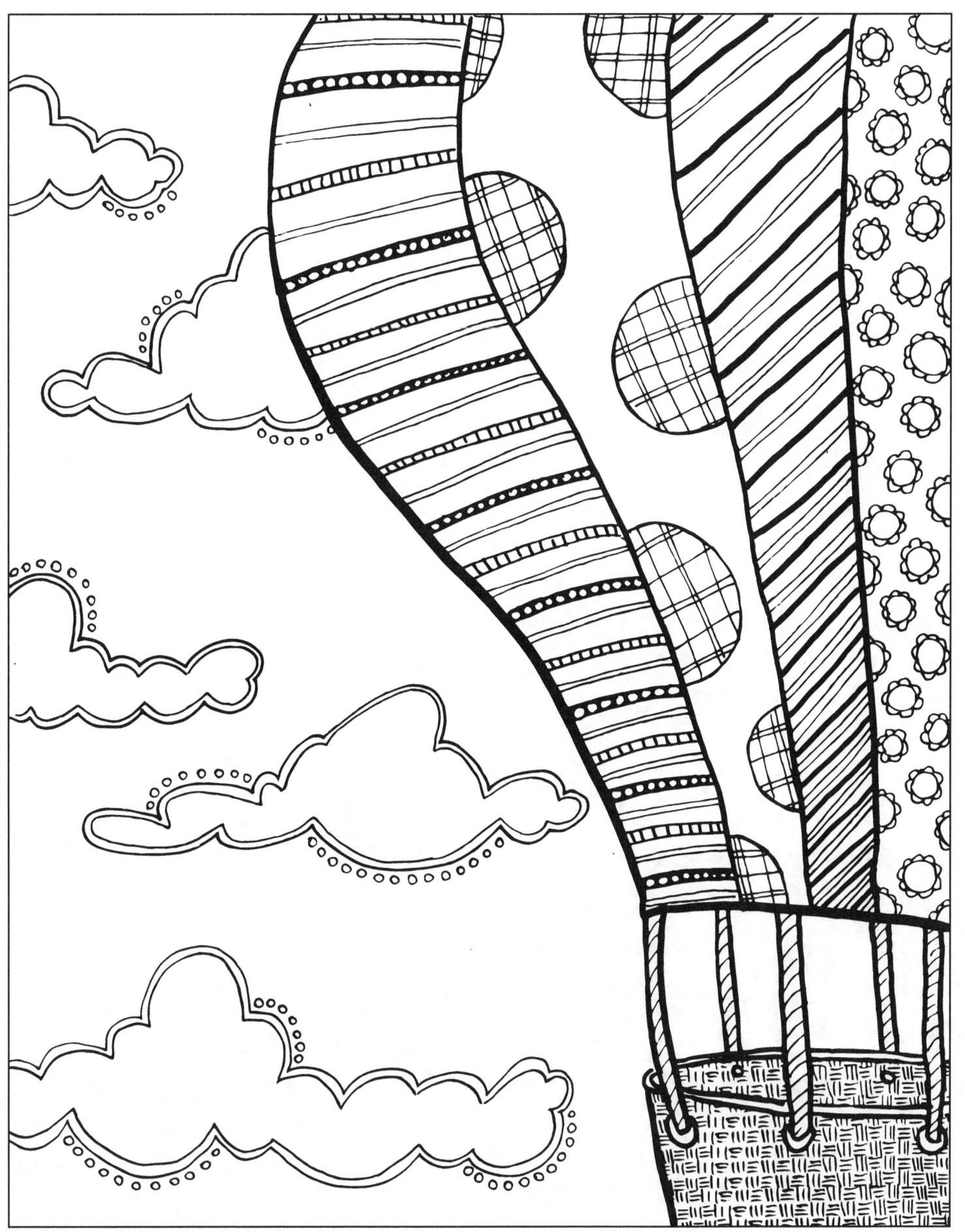

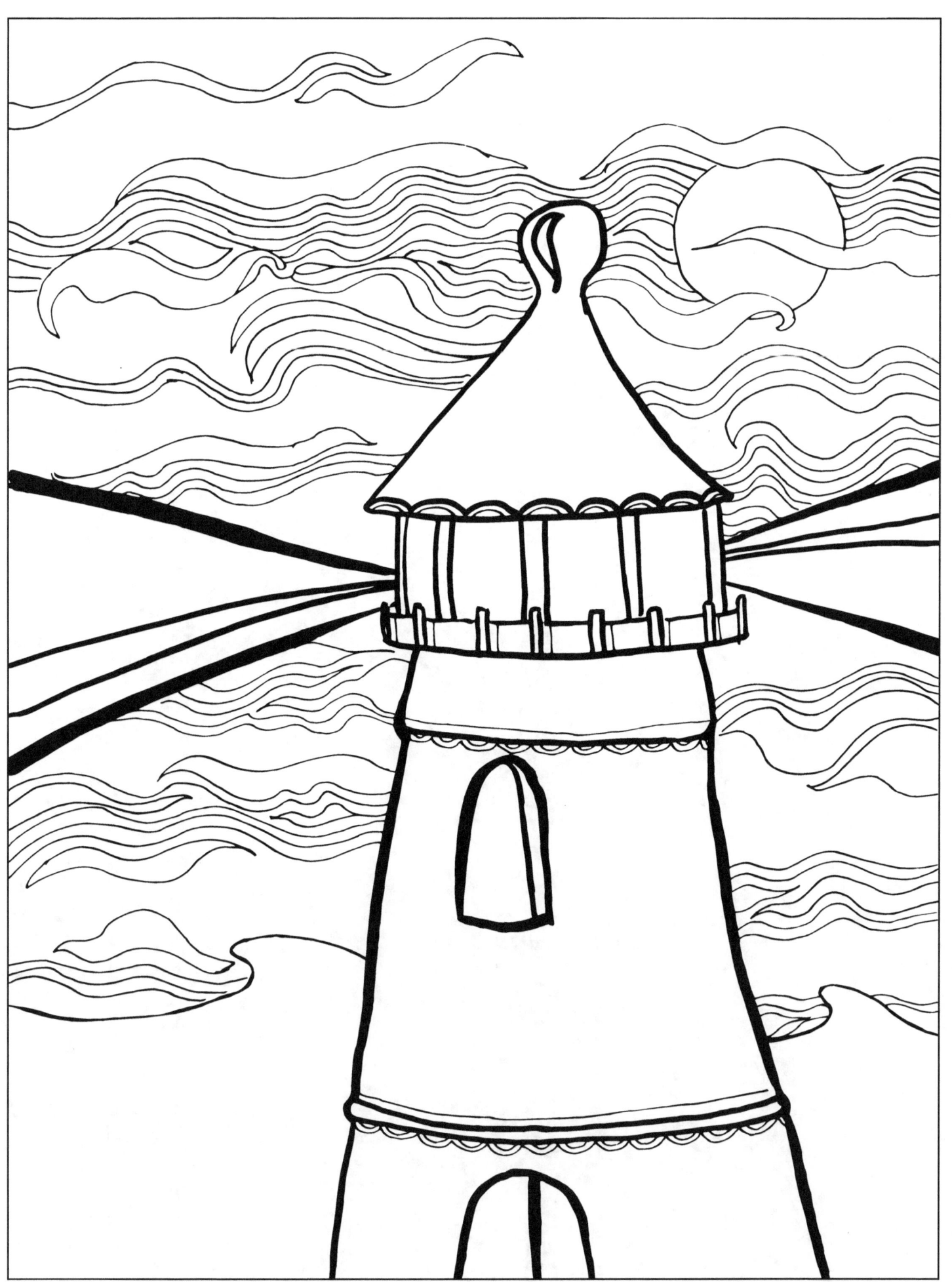

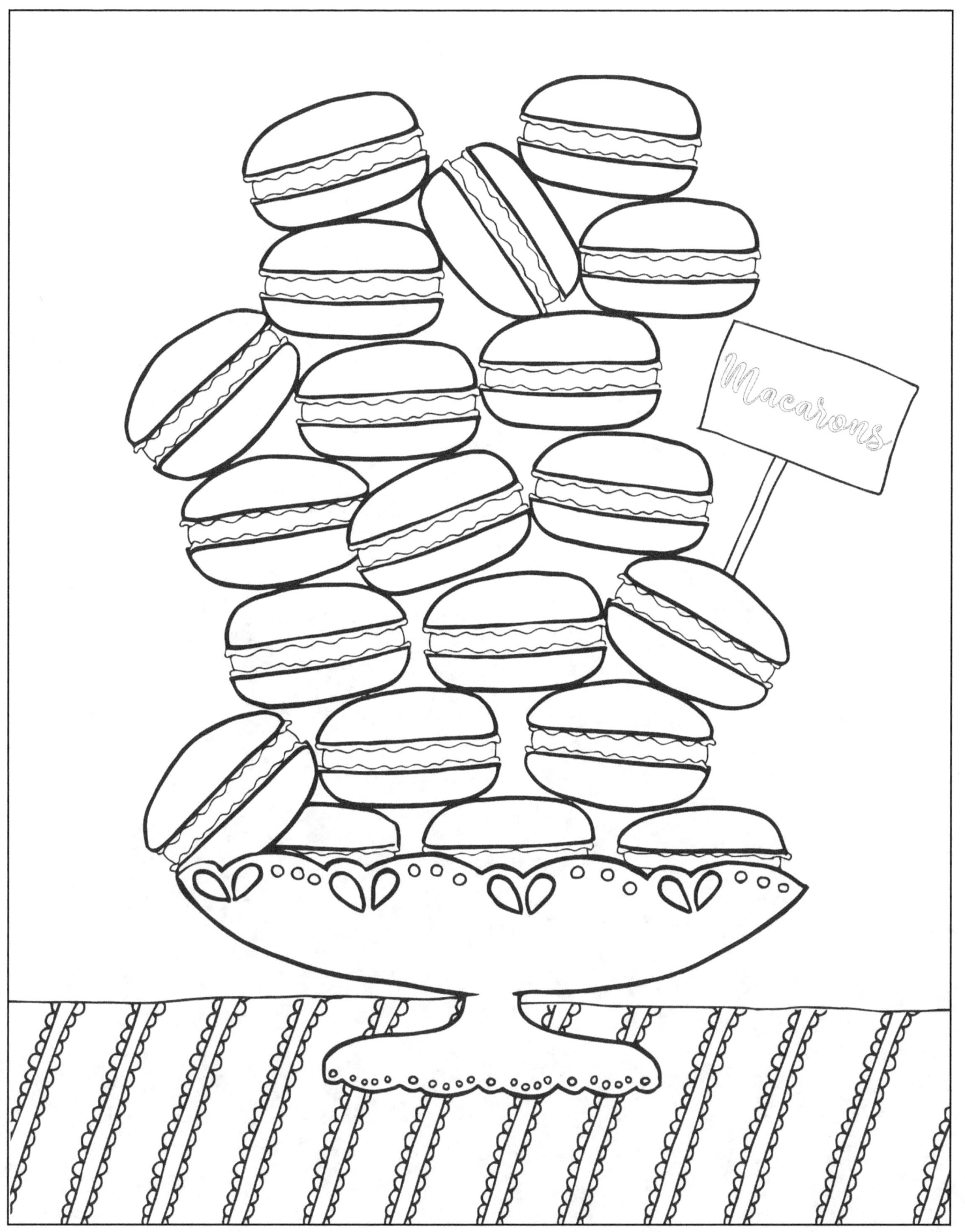

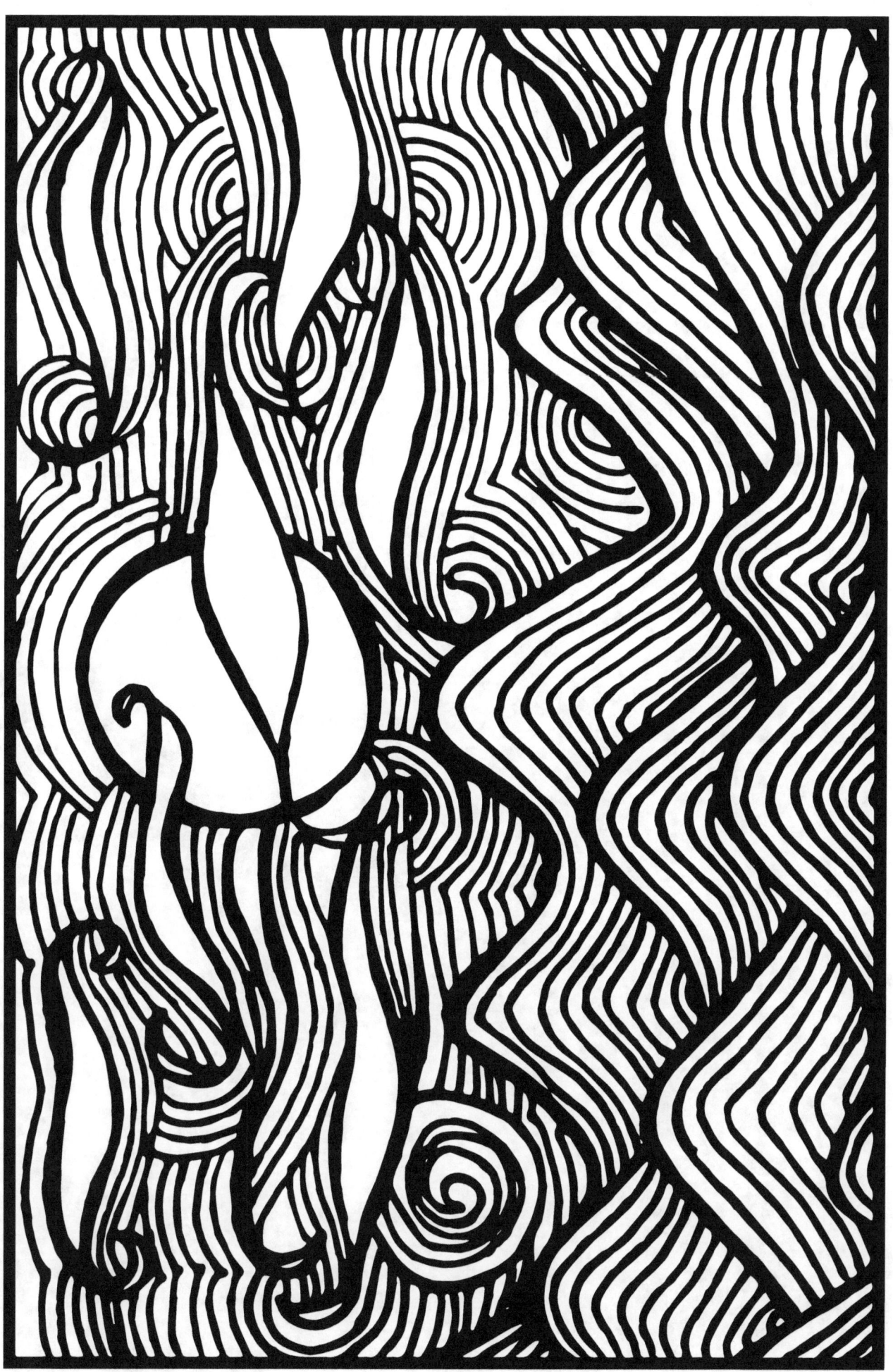

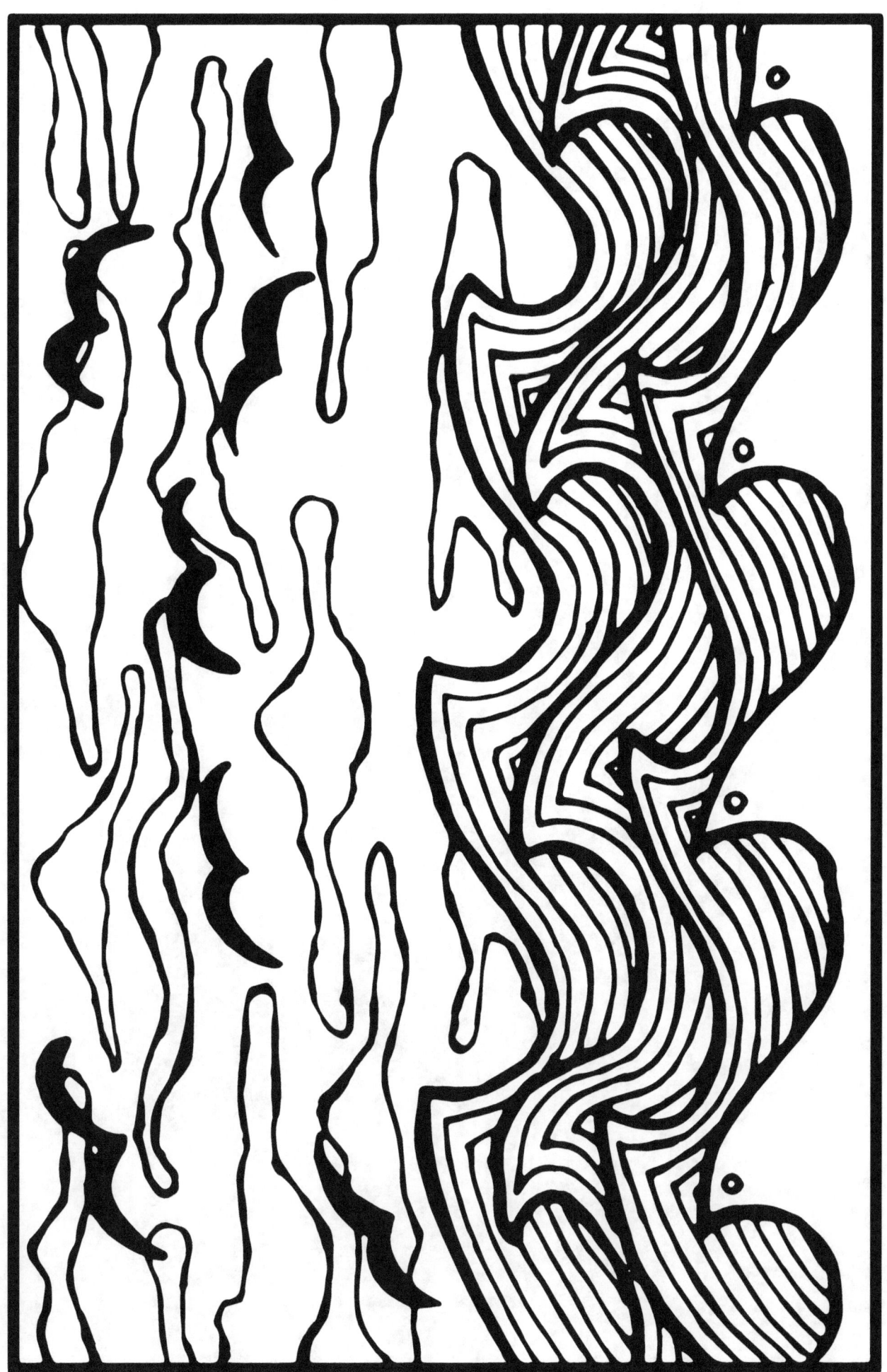

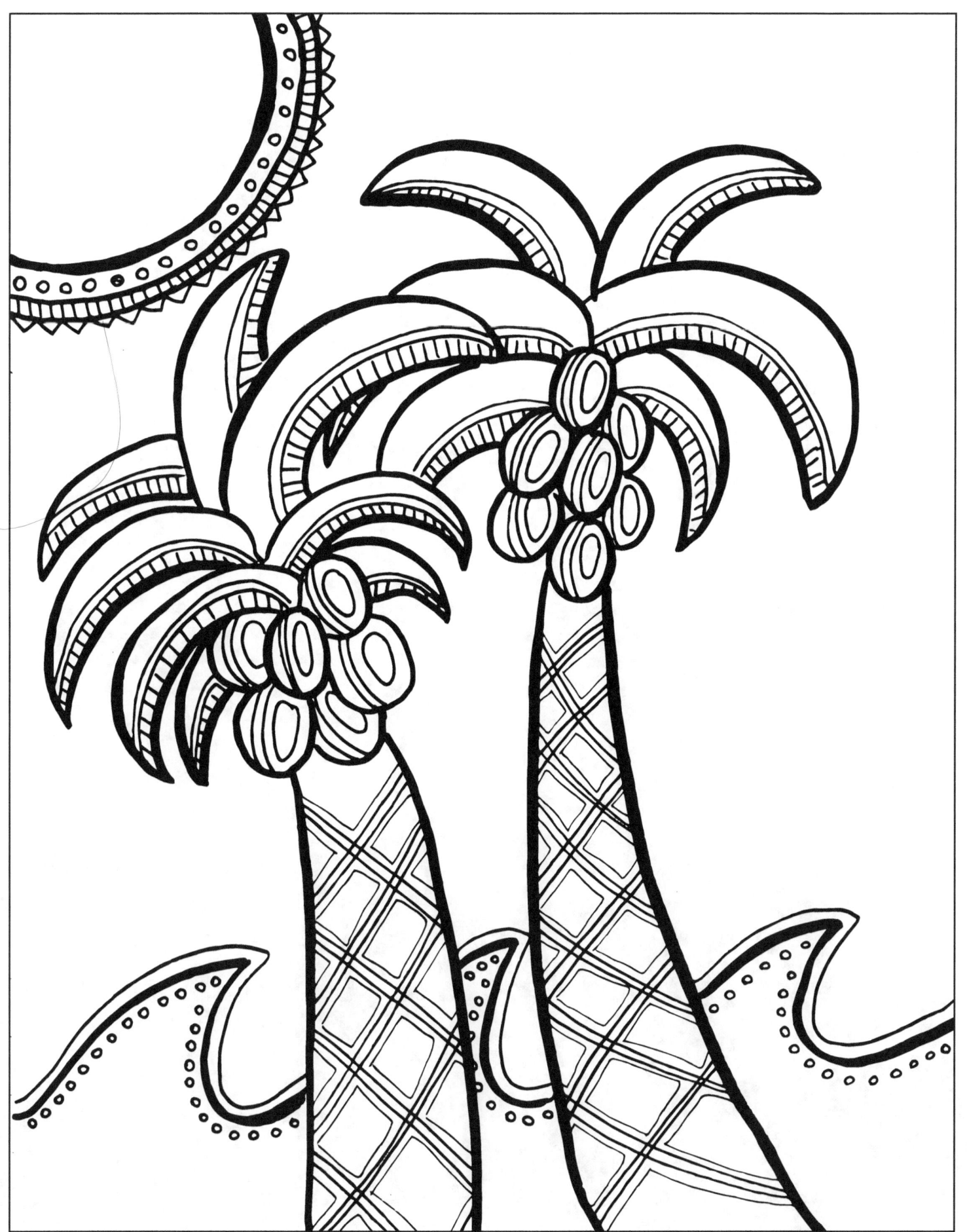

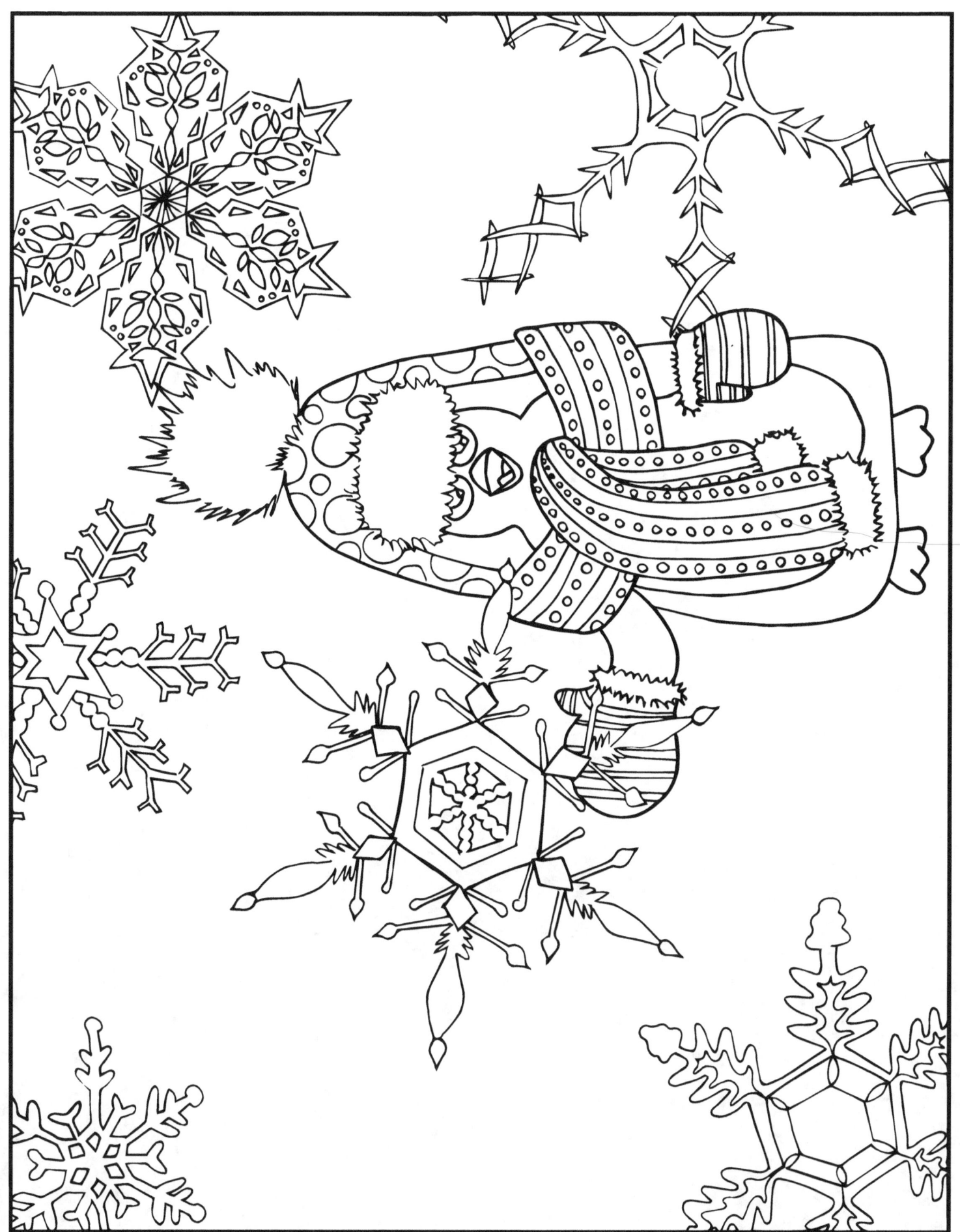

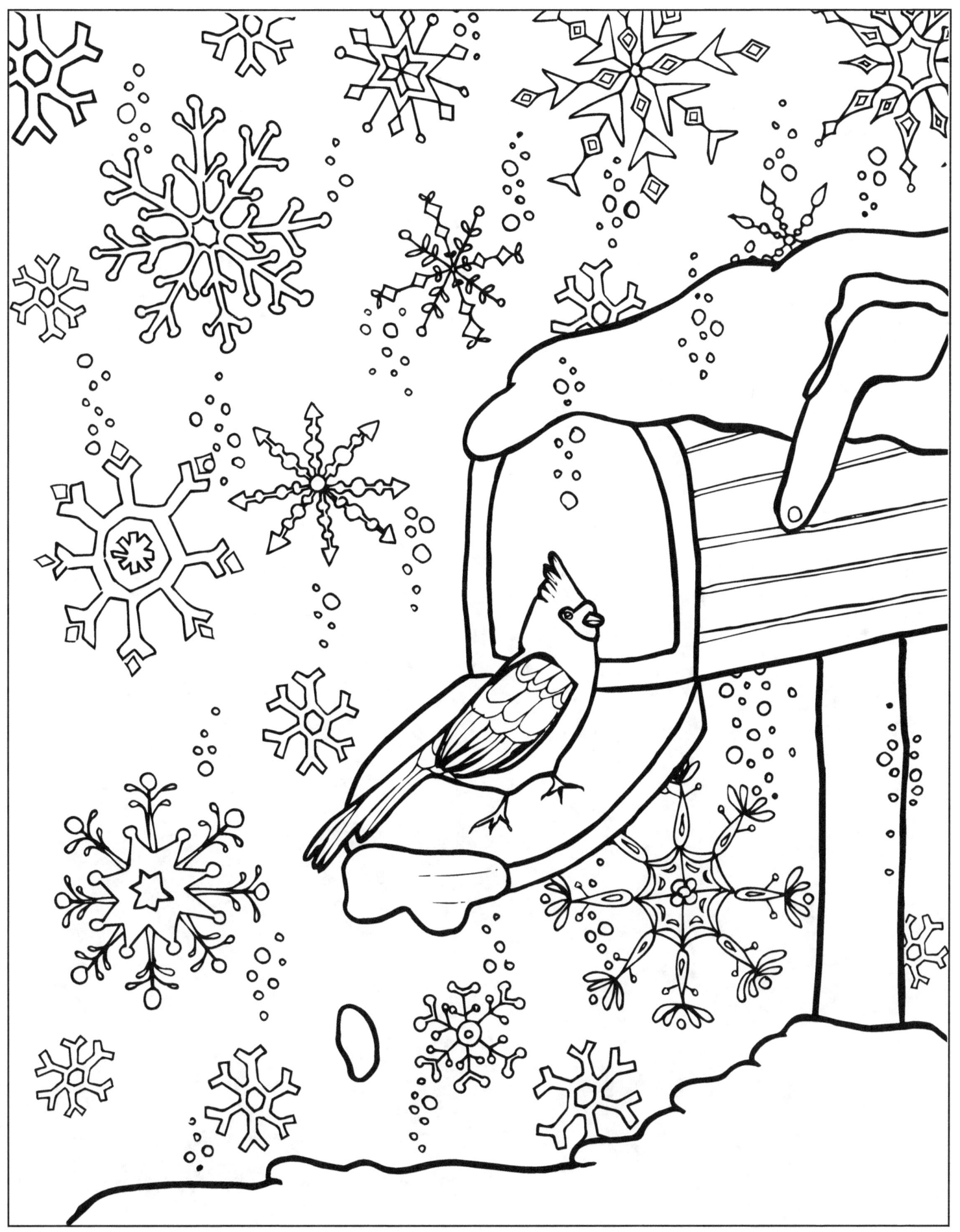

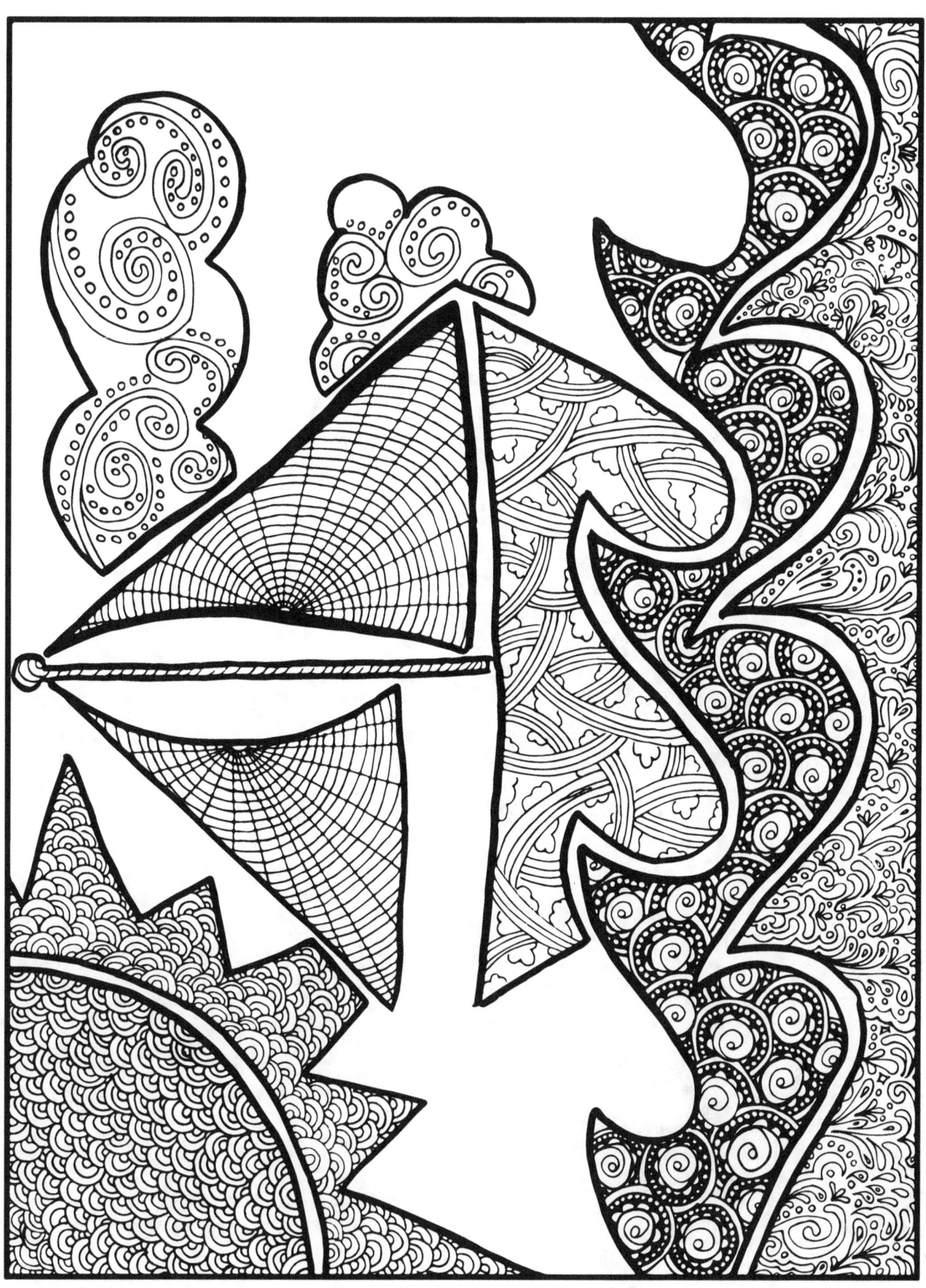

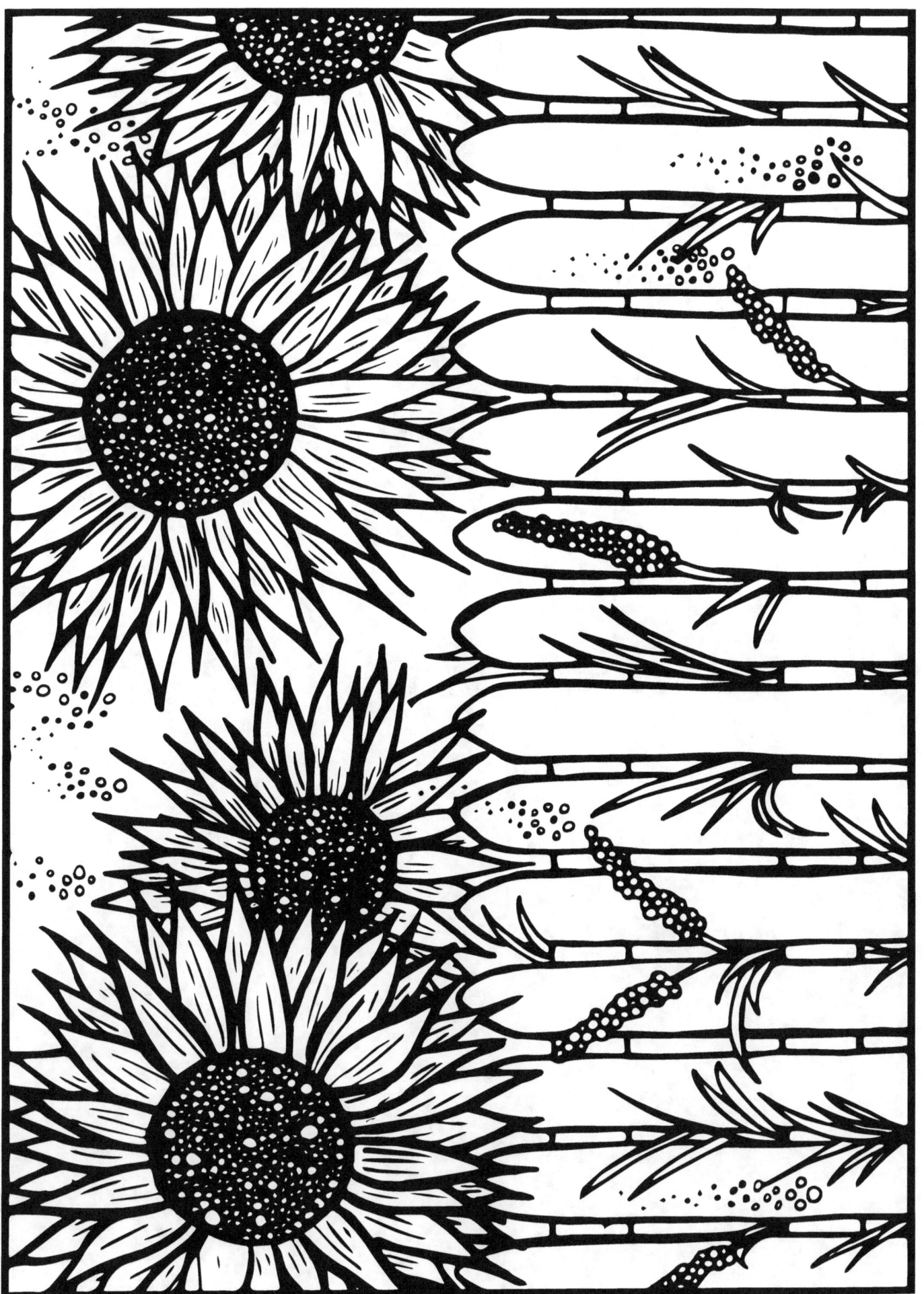

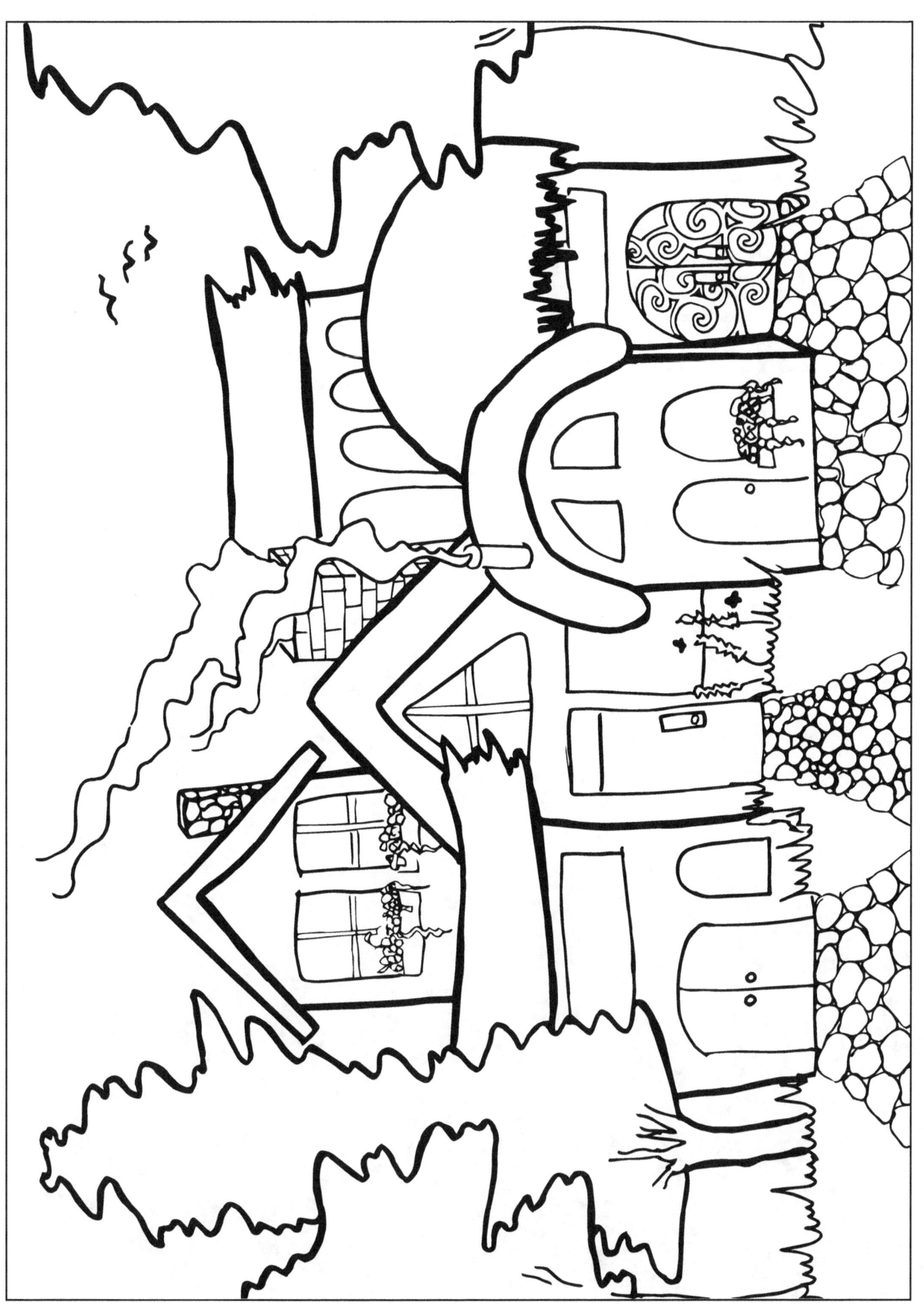

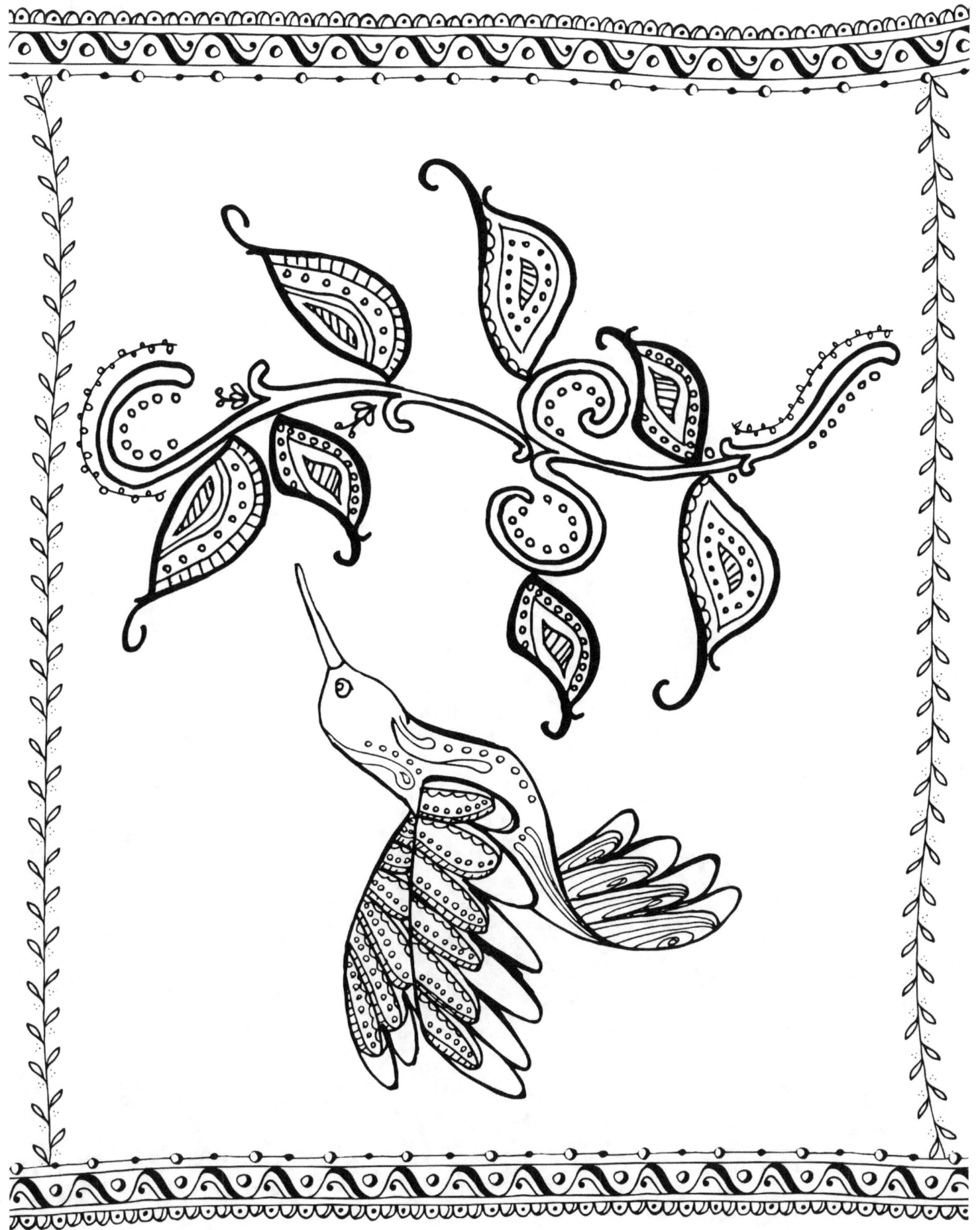

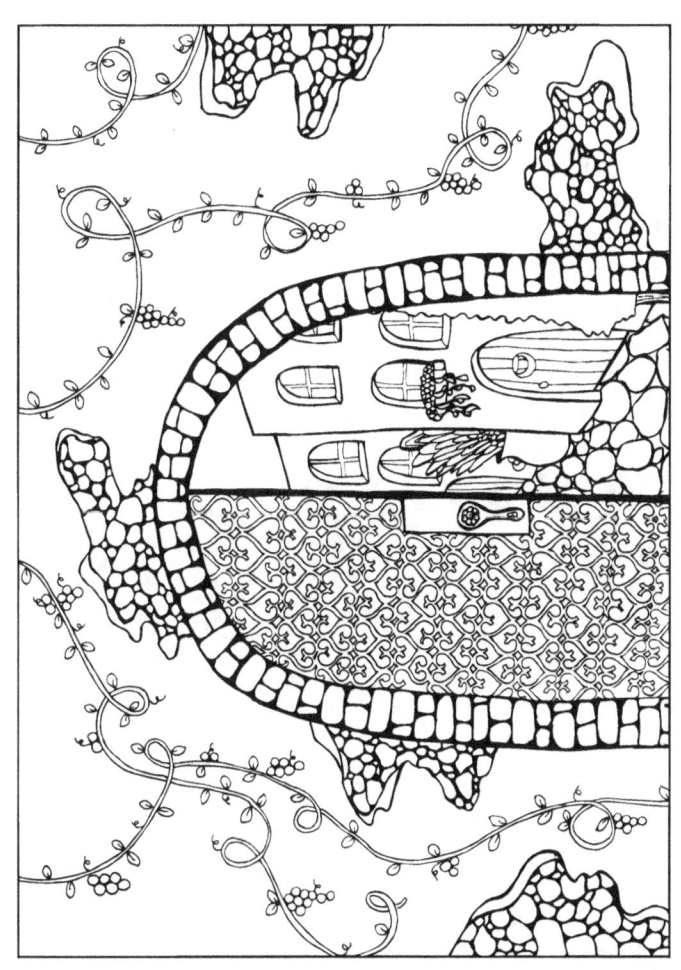
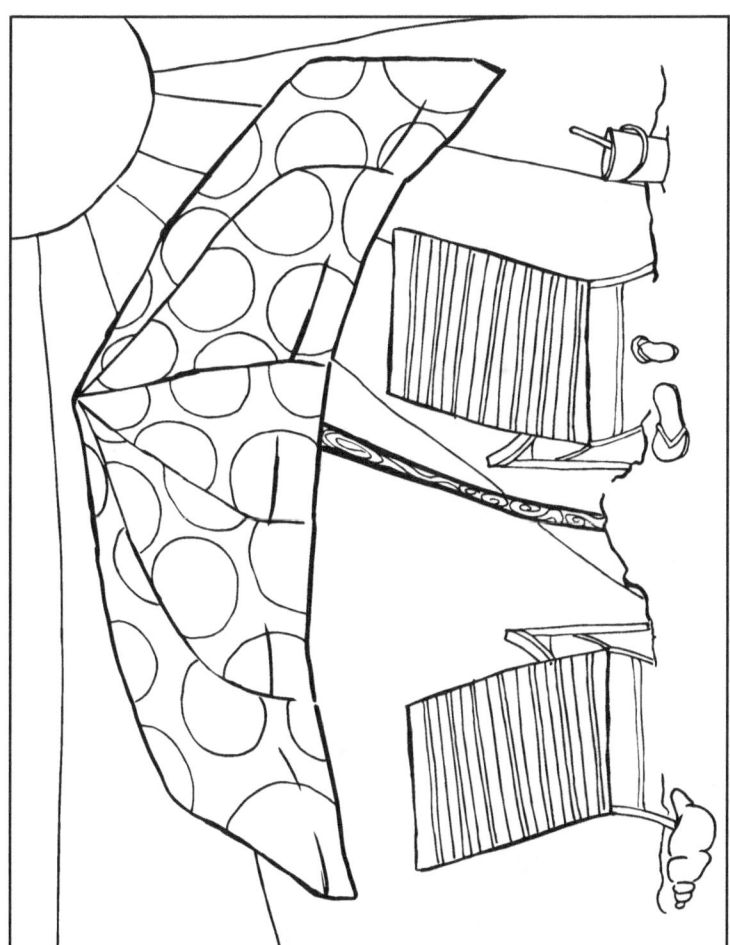
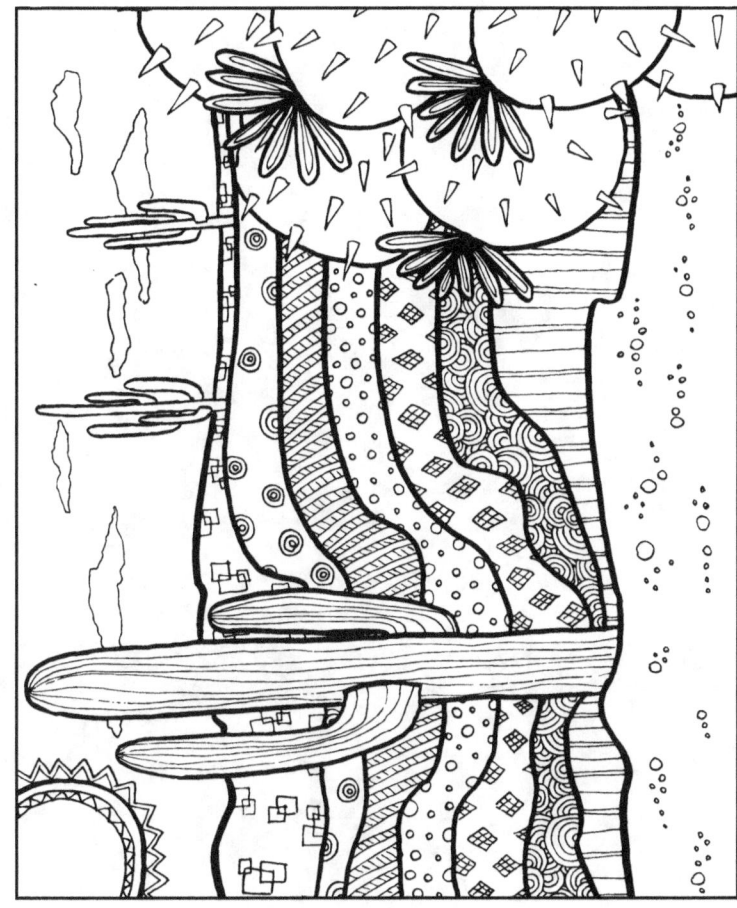
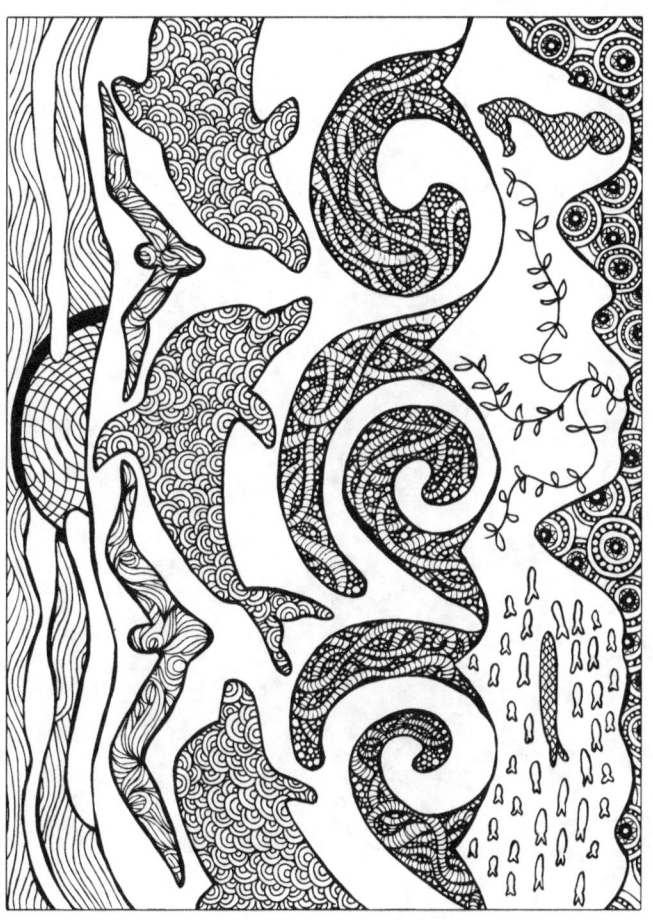

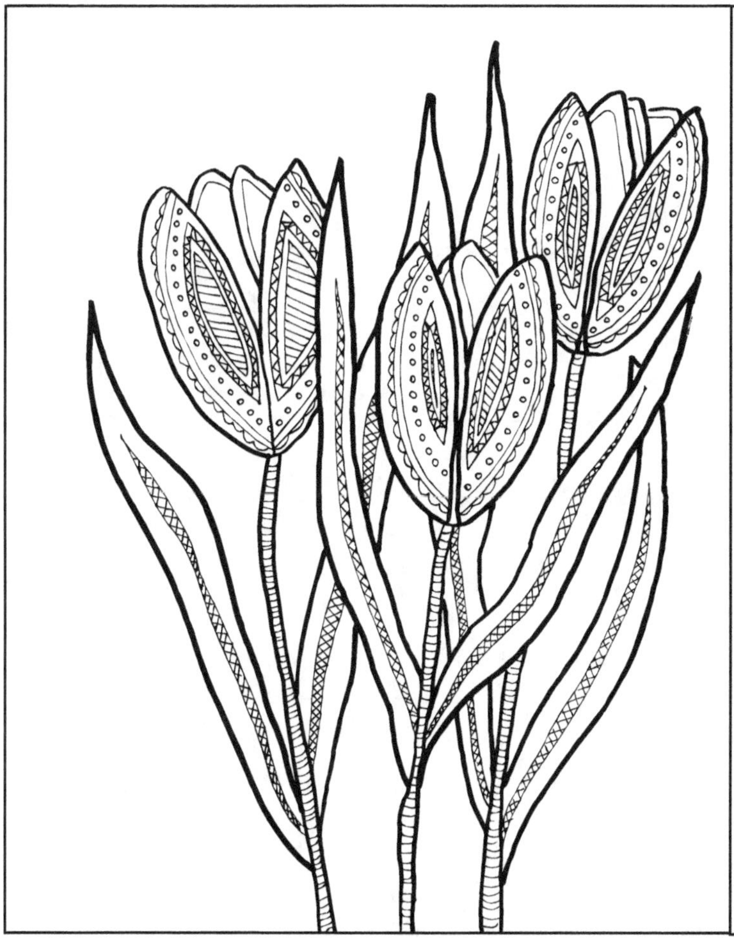

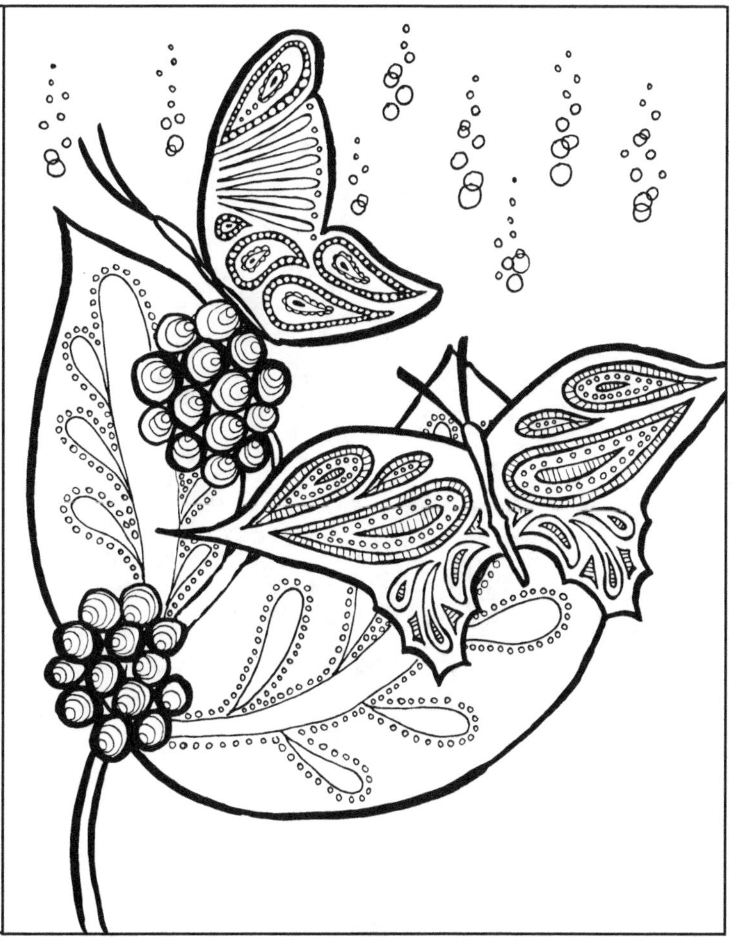

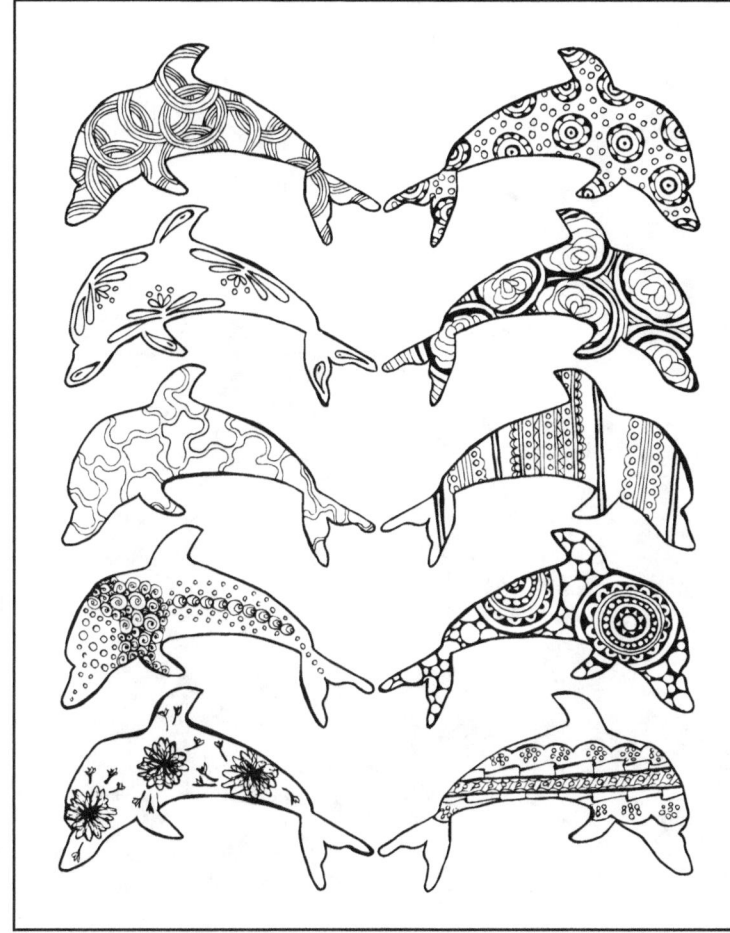
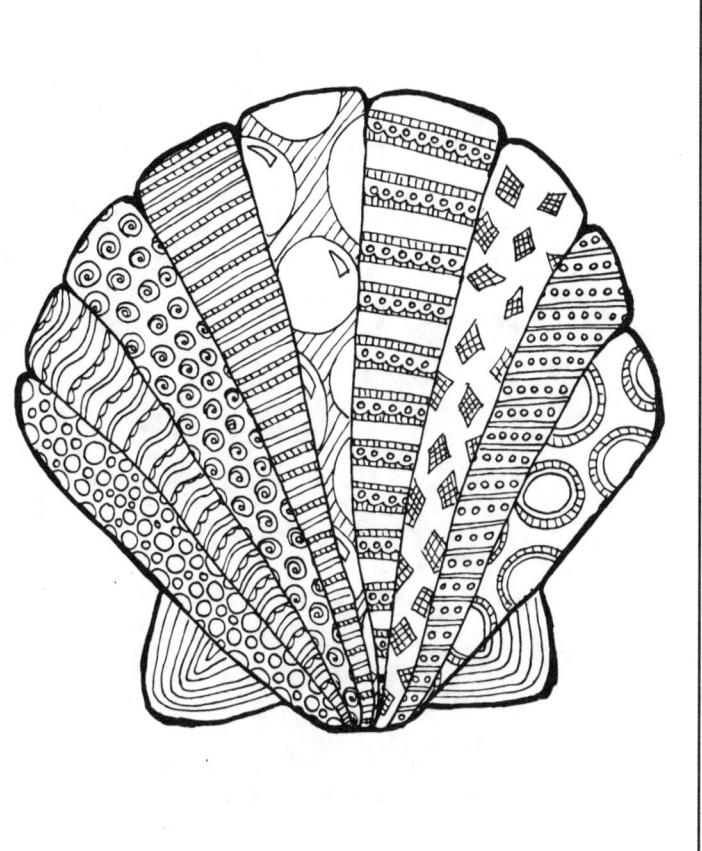

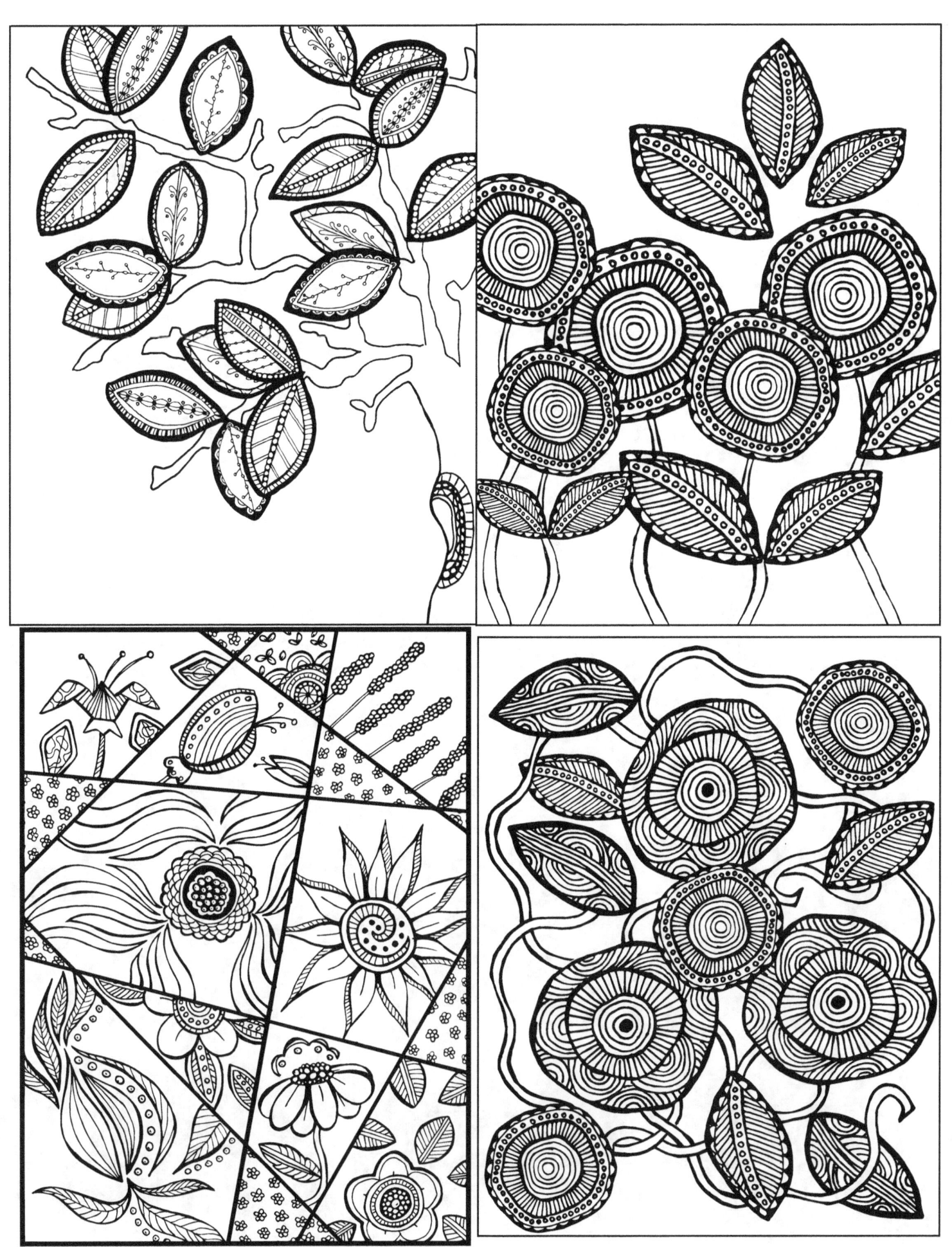

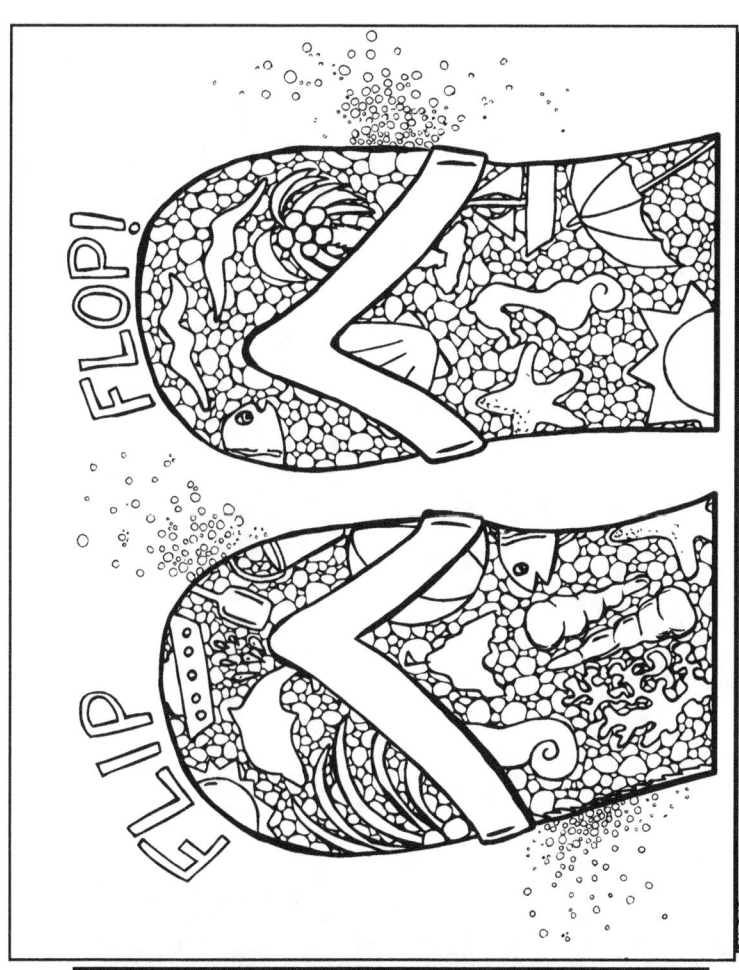

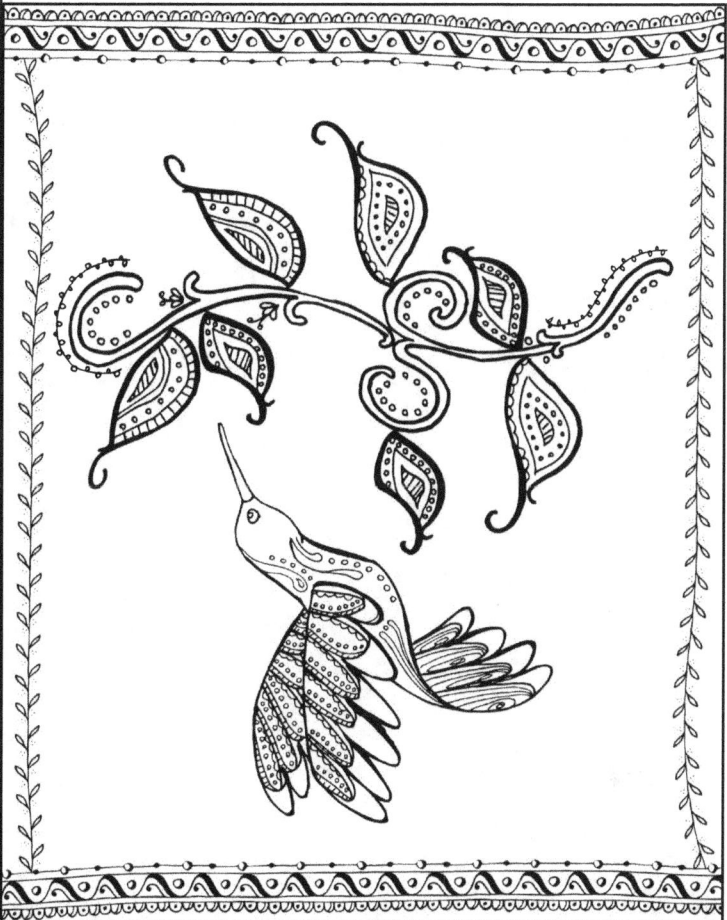

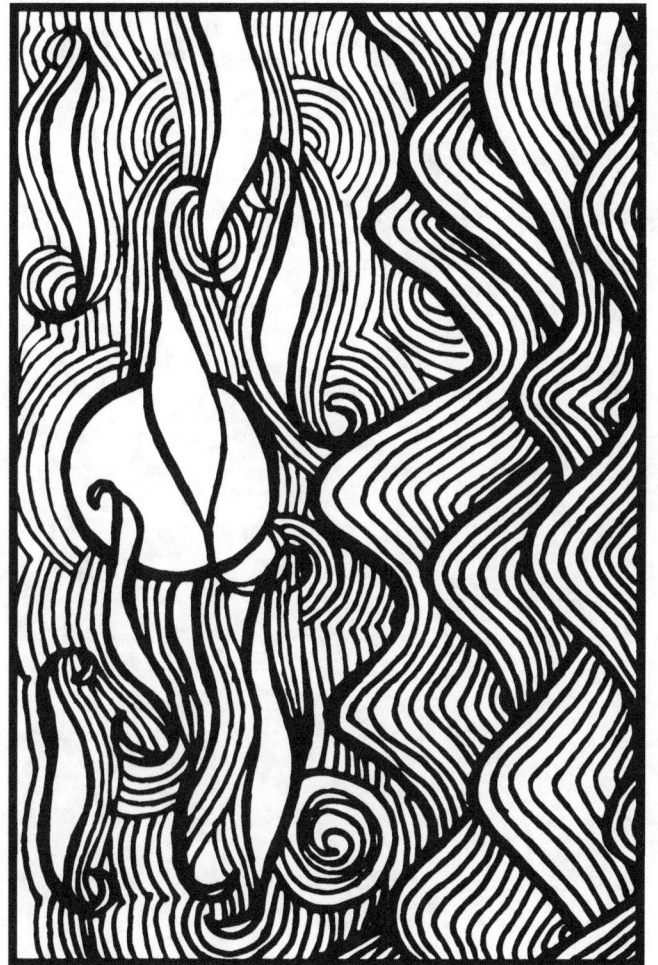

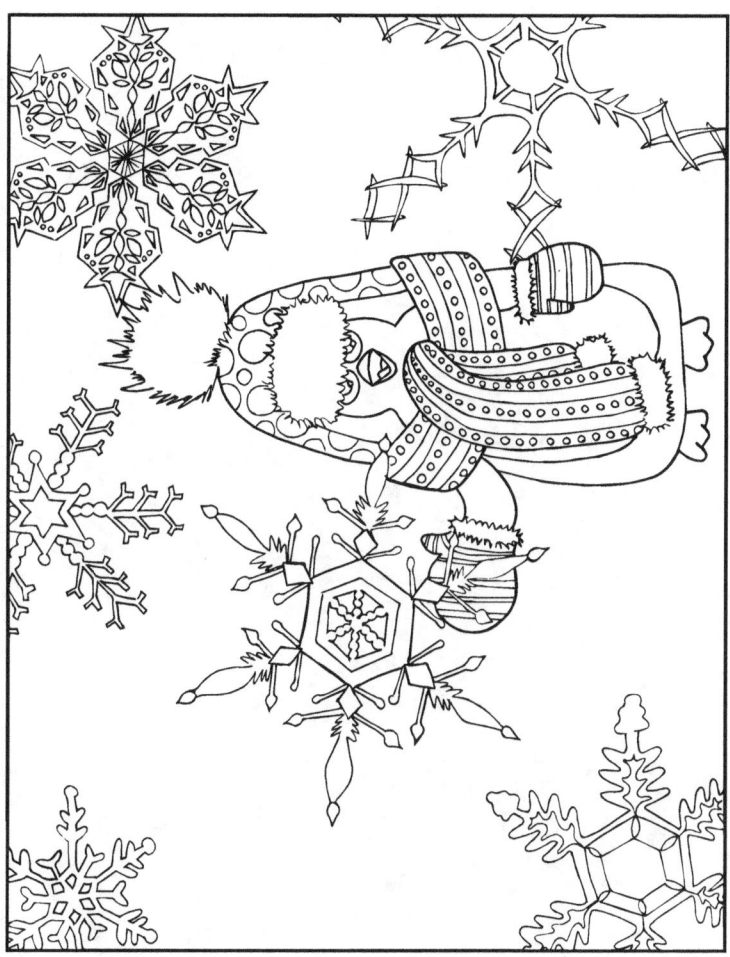

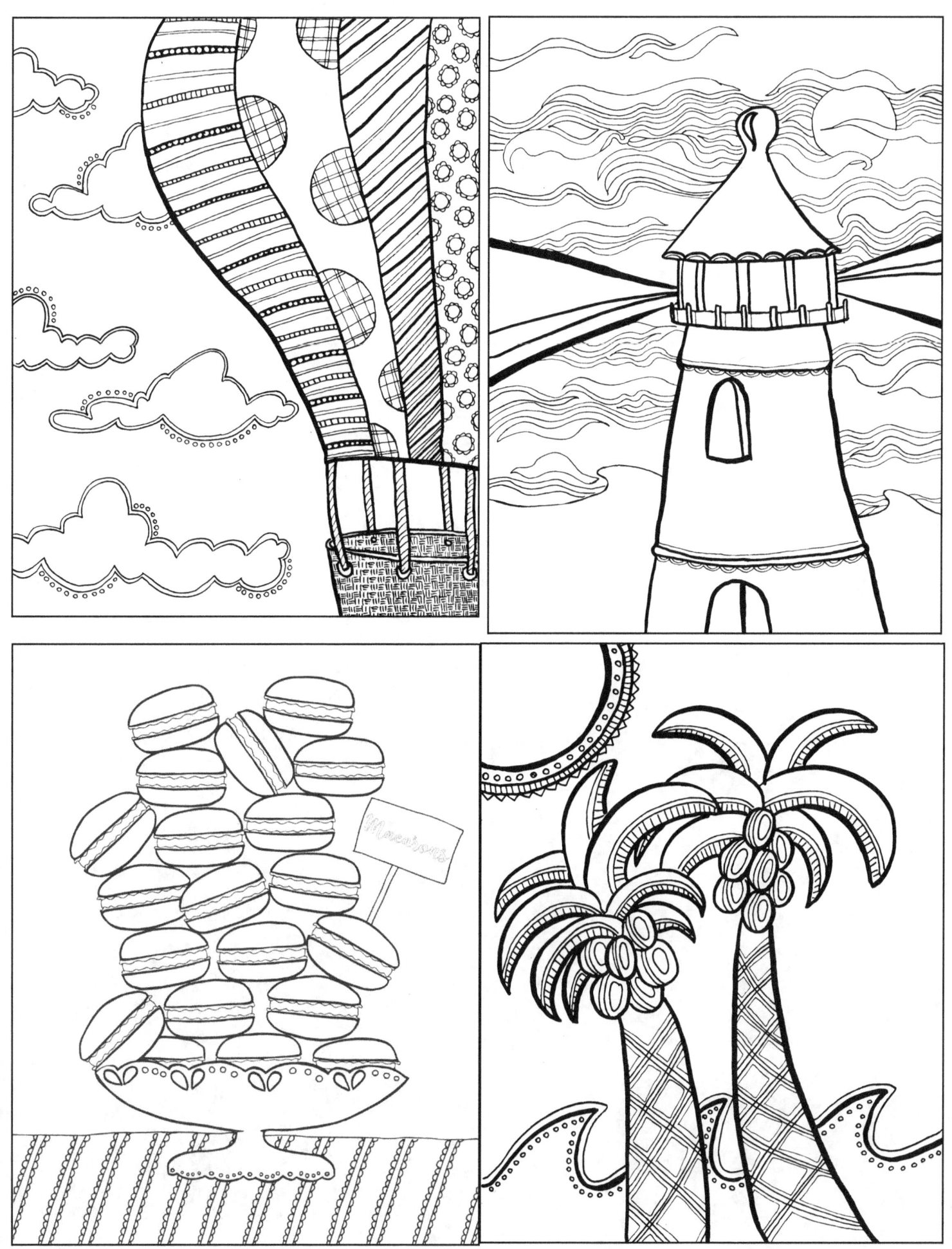

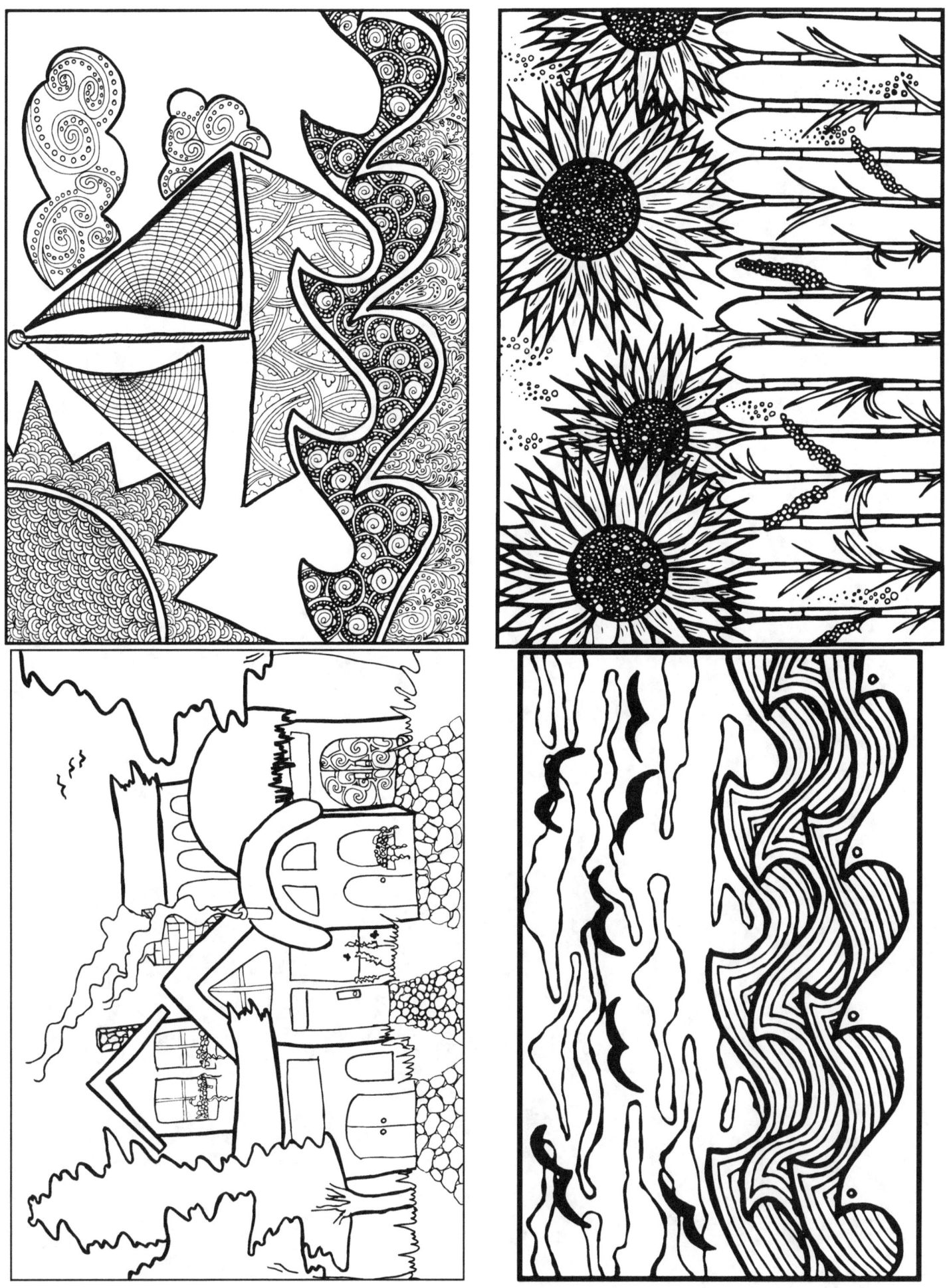

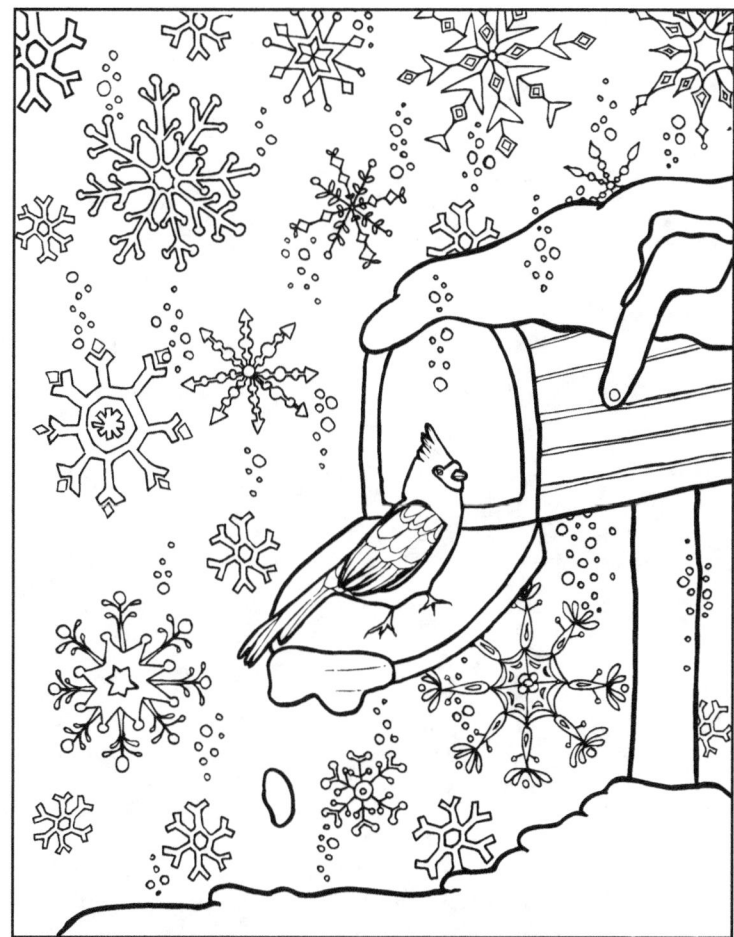

ABOUT THE ILLUSTRATOR

That's me!

I'm Menucha, just another creative like you. But I like to share my creativity with my world, and so I started my blog Moms & Crafters (momsandcrafters.com) after becoming a mom and deciding to stay home with my son...

The rest is history.

Today, I am lucky enough to work at home, illustrating, crafting, writing, and doing whatever else it is that us moms do... I have been blessed with two little boys, who keep me on my toes, and a vibrant community of blog readers.

I've published two previous coloring books, shown below, and authored the eBook *How to Build a Beautiful Blog* as well. Find my coloring books on Amazon (print), Etsy (digital) and Gumroad (digital). Find my eBook *How to Build a Beautiful Blog* on Gumroad.

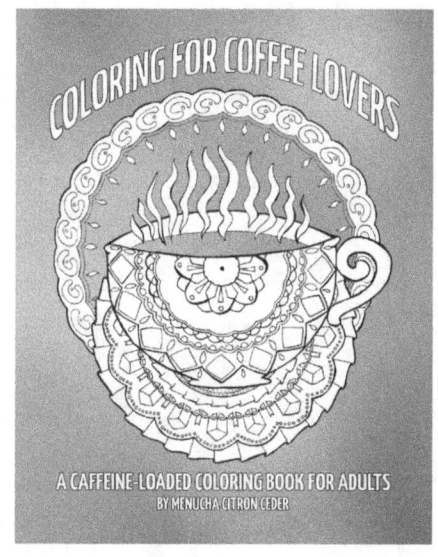

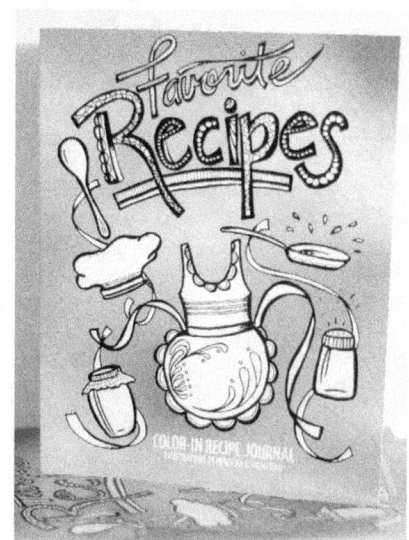

Tear out this page and place it behind the page you are coloring when using wet media, to act as a spacer in case of bleeding.

For more hand-drawn coloring pages for adults, The Color-in Recipe Journal, and Coloring for Coffee Lovers, visit momsandcrafters.com

www.ingramcontent.com/pod-product-compliance
Lightning Source LLC
Chambersburg PA
CBHW081014170526
45158CB00010B/3041